W9-CGM-794

SURVEY OF HISTORIC COSTUME
study guide

5th edition

PHYLLIS G. TORTORA

KEITH EUBANK

Vice President & General Manager, Fairchild Education & Conference Division: Elizabeth Tighe
Executive Editor: Olga T. Kontzias
Senior Associate Acquisitions Editor: Jaclyn Bergeron
Assistant Acquisitions Editor: Amanda Breccia
Editorial Development Director: Jennifer Crane
Development Editor: Noah Schwartzberg
Associate Development Editor: Lisa Vecchione
Creative Director: Carolyn Eckert
Production Director: Ginger Hillman
Senior Production Editor: Elizabeth Marotta
Copyeditors: Cate DaPron, Laurie Gibson
Assistant Ancillaries Editors: Amy Butler, Monica Lugo
Cover Design: Carolyn Eckert
Text Design: Carolyn Eckert, Andrea Lau
Text Layout: Andrea Lau
Production Intern: Shoshana Blum
Director, Sales & Marketing: Brian Normoyle

Copyright © 2011 Fairchild Books, A Division of Condé Nast.
All rights reserved. No part of this book covered by the copyright hereon may be reproduced or used
in any form or by any means—graphic, electronic, or mechanical, including photocopying, recording,
taping, or information storage and retrieval systems—without written permission of the publisher.

Library of Congress Catalog Card Number: 2010930499

ISBN: 978-1-60901-221-2

GST R 133004424

Printed in the United States of America

TP09

Table of Contents

About This Guide

Fairchild Book's Study Guide for *Survey of Historic Costume*, 5th edition, is designed to help you effectively navigate the text. The Study Guide is not a substitute for the text; but rather a tool to help you identify, synthesize, and retain the text's core information. In order to maximize the benefits of this Study Guide, use the activities presented in each chapter of the Guide to direct your reading. The key to success in its use will come from your attention to those areas your instructor emphasizes and the notes you take as you read.

Organized in Parts and Chapters parallel with the book, the Study Guide includes material directly related to all aspects of the text, as well as supplementary features such as illustrations, contemporary comments, and summary tables. Part openers provide a broad historical context and shed light on elements related to all of the periods covered in each Part.

For every chapter, the Study Guide includes the following sections:

- a concise **Historical Snapshot** to situate you in time;
- **space to take notes** about major content and themes;
- **questions** to help you identify this information in the text;
- **tables summarizing key information** about dress from the time period covered by each chapter;
- questions about the **relationship of decorative and fine arts to costume**;
- **activities** in which you must sketch or describe key styles; and
- **review questions**.

The Guide also contains a **Glossary**. The Glossary includes definitions of key costume terms from *Survey of Historic Costume*, 5th edition, as well as definitions of related arts movements.

The time period covered in studying the history of Western costume is measured not in hundreds but in thousands of years. The study of how people dressed is connected to all aspects of the civilization in which they lived. A text provides the informational foundation from which a course grows. Your instructor will provide guidance to any unique approaches to the study of historic costume your course will take. By providing a consistent approach to all of the chapters in this text, we hope we have provided a vehicle that enhances the journey you will take through time and place, making the contents accessible, memorable, and exciting.

CHAPTER ONE

Introduction

As you read Chapter 1 (pp. 1–11), make notes related to the areas identified below. These notes will help you understand how dress has been used by people throughout history.

1. According to the textbook, why do people wear clothes? (pp. 1–2)

2. What are the limits to the design of clothes? (pp. 2–3)

3. Explain (in your own words) what *theme* means as it is being used in the book. (p. 3)

4. List five themes presented in Chapter 1 and give examples from current fashion. (pp. 3–10)
    1.
    2.
    3.
    4.
    5

5. How does this book define *fashion*? (p. 8)

6. If you were researching historic costume, list five kinds of sources you could consult. (pp. 9–10)
    1.
    2.
    3.
    4.
    5.

The Ancient World c. 3000 B.C.–A.D. 300

Read pages 13–18 and complete the following chart.

	TIME PERIOD	PRESENT-DAY COUNTRIES OCCUPYING THIS TERRITORY
CHAPTER 2		
CHAPTER 3		
CHAPTER 4		

After reading pages 14–15, can you identify and describe the basic garment types common to most of the Ancient cultures discussed in Part One?

CHAPTER TWO

The Ancient Middle East c. 3500–600 B.C.

HISTORICAL SNAPSHOT

Founded by the people called the Sumerians, the first civilizations in the Middle East
were located in Mesopotamia, in the area of present-day Iraq. The Sumerian civilization
(3500–2500 B.C.) never developed a strong political organization, and its loose confederation
of states was conquered by the Amorites, who established a new empire with the capital
at Babylon. Following a period of expansion, Babylonian power began to decline, and the
Assyrians became the preeminent military force in the region until they were displaced by the
Chaldeans in 612 B.C. Chaldean Babylon, notable for its luxury and wealth, was the site of the
Hanging Gardens.

At the same time as the first Sumerian cities were built, the Nile River became the site of
Egyptian civilization. The ancient Egyptian kingdoms flourished from about 3200 B.C. until
about 300 B.C., when Greeks led by Alexander the Great conquered Egypt. As a result of
"indestructible" monuments and elaborate writing systems, details of the life and history of
Egypt are more complete than those of Mesopotamia over the same period.

MAJOR CONTENT AND THEMES OF THE ANCIENT MIDDLE EAST

As you read Chapter 2 (pp. 19–49), use the space provided to take notes about the chapter.
Focus your attention on those areas that your instructor identifies as important. Return to
Chapter 1, pages 3–10, and review the concept of theme as a unifying subject and idea related
to dress. Try to identify examples of dress that relate to the themes identified in the summary
on page 45. These notes will help you answer questions related to the key concepts and
learning objectives, and later prepare for tests and projects.

Based on your reading of Chapter Two and your notes about the Ancient Middle East, can you answer the following questions?

1. What are some of the major similarities and differences between Mesopotamian and Egyptian cultures? (pp. 21–22)

2. What are examples of how social life and social roles shaped clothing practices in Mesopotamian and Egyptian cultures? (pp. 22–45)

3. What was the primary fabric used in Mesopotamian textile production and why? (p. 23)
What was the primary fabric used in Egyptian textile production and why? (pp. 32–33)

4. Who was Herodotus? What did he learn about dress customs or restrictions related to religion in Ancient Egypt? (p. 35)

5. What aspects of Mesopotamian and Egyptian costume can be found in later historic periods? (pp. 47–48)

Mesopotamian/Sumerian Costume c. 3500–2500 B.C.

	GARMENTS (P. 24)	HAIR AND HEADDRESS (P. 24)	JEWELRY (P. 24)
MEN AND WOMEN	Skirts and full-body coverings Early-period dress made from fleece **kaunakes** Later period: woven cloth as well as belts and cloaks made from leather	Men depicted both clean shaven and bearded, sometimes with bald heads **Chignons** and **fillets** used by men and women to hold back long hair	Some royal women wear elaborate gold jewelry

Mesopotamian Costume/Later Sumerians and Babylonians c. 2500–1000 B.C.

	GARMENTS (P. 26)	HAIR AND HEADDRESS (P. 26)	FOOTWEAR (P. 26)	JEWELRY (P. 27)	MILITARY (P. 25)
MEN	Similar to early period, but with increasing complexity	Similar to early period	Bare feet are common The well-to-do wear sandals	Similar to early period	Skirts and shawls made of woven fabric. Leather or metal helmets
WOMEN	**Kaunakes** associated with religious figures Garments cut to cover entire body				

Mesopotamian Costume/Later Babylonians and the Assyrians c. 1000–600 B.C.

	GARMENTS (PP. 28–29)	HAIR AND HEADDRESS (PP. 29–30)	FOOTWEAR (PP. 29–30)	JEWELRY (PP. 29–30)	MILITARY (P. 29)	SPECIAL OCCASIONS (P. 28)
MEN	**Tunic**-style garments worn with a belt Royalty depicted with fringed shawls over the tunics Undergarments made from linen	Beards Hair arranged in curls **Fez** or **tarbush** hats	Sandals Closed shoes High boots on horsemen		Short tunics Mail made by sewing metal plates on fabric Helmets	Royalty wear floor-length tunics beneath embroidered shawls
WOMEN	Women's tunics have longer sleeves	Customs dictate wearing of veils	Sandals	Earrings, bracelets, and armlets		
CHILDREN (P. 30) **MESOPOTAMIAN COSTUME: C. 3500–600 B.C.**	Little known; probably minimal costume					

Egyptian Costume c. 3000–300 B.C.

	GARMENTS[A] (PP. 35–41)	HAIR AND HEADDRESS[B] (P. 42)	FOOTWEAR (P. 42)	JEWELRY (P. 42)	COSMETICS (P. 43)	MILITARY (P. 45)	RELIGIOUS (P. 45)
MEN	**Loincloth,** apron, **wrapped skirt, tunic,** shawls, and cloaks	Special religious headdress	High-status persons wear sandals	**Pectorals,** earrings, bracelets, armlets, and hair ornaments	Both men and women decorate their eyes, skin, and lips	Short skirts, padded leather helmets, and sleeveless leather corsets	Priests' costumes do not differ much from ordinary dress Special headdress religious and status-indentifying
WOMEN	Skirts, wrapped dress or sheath, bead-net dress, pleated and draped long dress, tunics, and V-necked dress	**Diadems** or fillets placed on the head held flowers		**Pectorals, amulets,** earrings, bracelets, armlets, and hair ornaments	Eye paint has cosmetic, symbolic, and medicinal use **Henna** used to color nails Scented ointments		The pharaoh appears wearing the special headdress or insignia of the gods
CHILDREN (PP. 43–45)	Minimal dress	Special hairstyles **Lock of Horus**		Bracelets, anklets, and earrings			

[A]For Eygptian garments, see Table 2.1, p. 34.

[B]For Eygptian headdress, see Illustrated Table 2.1, p. 44.

Relationship of Decorative and Fine Arts to Costume

Looking back at the "Decorative and Fine Arts Table" on page 16, choose one figure and describe how it relates to costume from this chapter.

Using the textbook and the "At a Glance" feature of Chapter Two of this study guide, can you sketch or describe the dress of the following people from the Ancient Middle East?

1. Sumerian man, c. 2200 B.C.

2. Sumerian woman of the period from 2500 to 1000 B.C.

3. Assyrian king of the period c. 1000–600 B.C.

4. Egyptian man of the New Kingdom Period

5. Egyptian woman of the Middle Kingdom Period

6. Egyptian soldier

7. The headdress of an Egyptian prince

1. How did the predominant use of different textile fibers in Mesopotamia and in Egypt contribute to the unique characteristics of the garments worn in each of these civilizations?

2. Compare the sources of information about costume in Mesopotamia and in Egypt. What are the major sources of information about costume in each of these civilizations? What limitations do these sources impose on understanding the costume of each civilization?

3. How can the dress of upper-class Egyptians as depicted in art be distinguished from that of lower-class Egyptians? What are some of the items of dress in Egypt that signified status?

4. Identify examples of elements of Mesopotamian and Egyptian costume that are thought to have come from another culture. What is thought to be their origin? What evidence can be cited to support the hypothetical origin?

5. Were there any distinctive aspects of children's clothing in either of the civilizations discussed in this chapter? What generalization can be made about clothing for children in the periods covered in Chapter 2? (p. 22 – 45)

NOTES

CHAPTER THREE

Crete and Greece c. 2900–300 B.C.

HISTORICAL SNAPSHOT

Minoan civilization flourished c. 2100–1100 B.C. During the Middle Period of Minoan civilization, 2100–1600 B.C., the Minoans maintained political control over Crete and what is today mainland Greece. The mainland people, called Mycenaeans, gradually grew stronger and by 1400 B.C. dominated the region. At the beginning of the 13th century, after a series of devastating attacks by invaders, Mycenaean civilization disappeared, and Greece entered a Dark Age about which little is known. As the Dark Age ended, Greece entered a so-called Archaic Period, c. 650–80 B.C. Independent city-states developed, and in the Classical Age (c. 500–323 B.C.) Greece enjoyed one of the most creative eras in the history of civilization. Greece established colonies and spread its influence throughout the Mediterranean world. As Greek influence waned after c. 300 B.C., Romans supplanted Greeks as the dominant force in the area.

MAJOR CONTENT AND THEMES IN THE DRESS OF CRETE AND GREECE

As you read Chapter 3 (pp. 51–72), use the space provided to take notes about the chapter. Focus your attention on those areas that your instructor identifies as important. Return to Chapter 1, pages 3–10, and review the concept of *theme* as a unifying subject and idea related to dress. Try to identify examples of dress that relate to the themes identified in the summary on page 70. These notes will help you answer questions related to the key concepts and learning objectives, and later prepare for tests and projects.

Based on your reading of Chapter Three and your notes about Crete and Greece, can you answer the following questions?

1. What technologies made possible the wide variety of Minoan and Grecian ornamental fabrics? (p. 53)

2. What major CROSS-CULTURAL FACTORS influenced Minoan and Greek dress? (pp. 54–55, 57–58, 70–71)

3. How did some of the variations in the forms of the **chiton** illustrate POLITICS and SOCIAL VALUES? (pp. 62–63)

4. What are some of the notable similarities between Greek arts and Greek dress? (pp. 61–62, 71–72)

5. To what does the Greek historian Herodotus attribute the change in style from the **Doric chiton** to the **Ionic chiton**? (pp. 63–64) To which theme listed on pages 70–71 does this relate?

Minoan Costume 2900–1100 B.C.

	GARMENTS (PP 53-56	OTHER GARMENTS (PP	HAIR AND HEADDRESS (P 56)	FOOTWEAR (P 56)	JEWELRY (P 56)	COSMETICS AND GROOMING (P 56)	SPECIAL OCCASION (PP 50, 53, 54)
MEN	Some tailored, some fitted clothing **Perizo ma** Wrapped skirts, both short and longer Long or short tunics	Poncho-like capes Shawls Tight, rolled belts	Long, curly hair or short, cut close to head Elaborate hat styles Including fillets, crown-like, turbans, caps, wide-brimmed hats	Sandals Ankle high shoes with pointed toes	Rings, bracelets, armlets	Clean-shaven	Reinforced loincloths worn for bull-leaping sport by men and women
WOMEN	Bell-shaped skirts, some flared, some with ruffles, others shape unclear Sheep fleece skirts Bodice fitted, some examples open to leave breasts exposed Long tunics Apron over skirt	Shawls Later period women wore tight rolled belts	Long, curly hair Held in place by fillet or jeweled bands		Rings, bracelets, armlets Necklaces	Eye makeup Perhaps lip color	
CHILDREN	Probably simple skirts or tunics Dressed as adults at puberty						

Greek Costume 650–300 B.C.

	GARMENTS (PP. 62–64)	OTHER GARMENTS (PP. 64–65)	HAIR (P. 65)	HEADDRESS (P. 65)	FOOTWEAR (P. 67)	JEWELRY (P. 67)	SPECIAL OCCASIONS (P. 68)	MILITARY (P. 69)	THEATRICAL (P. 70)
MEN	**Chiton** **Himation**	**Perizoma** **Chlamys**	Archaic Period: long or medium-length hair, beards predominate Classical Period: young men wear short hair and no beards, and older men wear longer hair and beards	**Petasos** **Phrygian bonnet**	Sandals			**Greaves** **Cuirass**	Use of masks, significant dress, insignias, and color
WOMEN	**Chiton** **Himation**	**Diplax** **Chlamydon**	Archaic Period: women wear their hair long, in curling tresses, with curls around the face Classical Period: hair pulled back in knot, or **chignon**	Fillets, scarves, ribbons, and caps	Sandals	Necklaces, earrings, decorative fastening pins	Female wedding attire: **Hercules knot, stephane,** and **nymphides**		
CHILDREN (PP. 67–68)	**Swaddling clothes** for infants Girls and boys wear **chitons** and **himations**		Small children and boys wear short hair Older girls wear their hair like women	Flat-crowned hat with heavy brim	Barefoot				

Relationship of Decorative and Fine Arts to Costume

Looking back at the "Decorative and Fine Arts Table" on page 16, choose one figure and describe how it relates to costume from this chapter.

Using the textbook and the "At a Glance" feature of Chapter Three of this study guide, can you sketch or describe the dress of the following people from Crete and Greece?

1. Man of Crete

2. Woman of Crete

3. Man of Archaic Greece

4. Woman of Archaic Greece

5. Man of Classical Greece who is dressed to travel

6. Woman of Classical Greece wearing an **Ionic chiton**

7. Woman of Classical Greece wearing a **Hellenistic chiton**

8. Greek soldier

1. In what ways can the form of Minoan costume be said to be quite different from that of the Mesopotamian and Egyptian civilizations and from that of the later Greek periods?

2. Experts are unsure about the cut of certain elements of Minoan women's costume. What are the alternative explanations for the cut of women's bodices and for the skirt style depicted in Figure 3.4? (p. 55) Why are these features unclear?

3. What ornamentation techniques were employed by Minoan weavers? Were these techniques adopted by the Mycenaeans or by the Greeks of the Archaic period?

4. Distinguish between the **Doric peplos**, **chitoniskos**, the **Ionic chiton**, the **Doric chiton**, and the **Hellenistic chiton**. What are some of the events or factors that are said to have resulted in the evolution of these styles?

5. What are the major sources of information about Greek costume in the Archaic, Classical, and Hellenistic periods? What has contributed to misunderstandings about the Greek use of color?

6. What evidence can be found in Greek textiles of trading contacts with the Far East?

7. What are some of the factors that resulted in the extension of Greek influence subsequent to the Greek period? In what areas did Greek influences continue?

8. What is swaddling? What reason might the Greeks have had for swaddling? When and where else was it used?

9. How are certain elements of Greek wedding dress related to the theme of GENDER ROLES in Greek society?

CHAPTER FOUR

Etruria and Rome c. 800 B.C.–A.D. 400

HISTORICAL SNAPSHOT

The Etruscan culture that developed along the Italian peninsula by about 800 B.C. was superior in skills and artistic production to neighboring tribes. Gradually a confederation of Etruscan city-states gained control of large areas. Greek colonies were established in Sicily and in some locations on the Italian peninsula. A local tribe that later took the name Romans steadily grew stronger, and by about the 3rd century B.C. the Etruscans were subjugated by the Romans.

Kings ruled Rome until the formation of a Republic in 509 B.C. Under the Republic, Rome gained control of all of Italy; much of North Africa; and large parts of the Middle East, Eastern Europe, and continental Europe. Augustus, the successor to the assassinated Julius Caesar, established the Roman Empire in 27 B.C., adding more territory. After 200 years of prosperity and relative peace, the Empire began to decline after the 3rd century A.D. The capital was moved east to Constantinople in A.D. 325. An emperor for the Eastern or Byzantine Empire was named in 395 and another for Rome, and by 476 the Roman emperor was deposed by barbarians, thus ending the Roman Empire, while the ByzantineEmpire flourished.

MAJOR CONTENT AND THEMES OF ETRURIA AND ROME

As you read Chapter Four (pp. 75–97), use the space provided to take notes about the chapter. Focus your attention on those areas that your instructor identifies as important. Return to Chapter 1, pages 3–10, and review the concept of *theme* as a unifying subject and idea related to dress. Try to identify examples of dress that relate to the themes identified in the summary on page 94. These notes will help you answer questions related to the key concepts and learning objectives, and later prepare for tests and projects.

Based on your reading of Chapter Four and your notes about Etruria and Rome, can you answer the following questions?

1. Etruscan art shows the unique aspects of Etruscan costume and Etruscan life. Where can this art be found? (p. 77)

2. List examples from the chapter that support the statements on pages 94–95 about how Etruscan dress can be said to illustrate the theme of CROSS-CULTURAL DRESS.

3. Note some examples that show that the Romans used their clothing as a way of demonstrating their SOCIAL STATUS. (p. 81)

4. Where did Romans obtain their clothing, and what textiles were most commonly used in their clothes? (pp. 81–82)

5. In what ways do Greek, Etruscan, and Roman costume differ? (p. 94)

6. How does the advice the Roman poet Ovid gives to men differ from that which he gives to women? (p. 85)

7. According to the textbook, what do contemporary fashion designers generally mean when they speak of "toga style"? (pp. 95–96)

Etruscan Costume 800–200 B.C.

	GARMENTS (PP. 77–78)	HAIR (P. 79)	HEADDRESS (P. 79)	FOOTWEAR (P. 80)	JEWELRY (P. 80)	SPECIAL OCCASIONS (P. 79)
MEN	**Perizoma** **Chiton** **Tebenna**	Archaic Period: medium-length hair, pointed beards Post- Archaic Period: short hair, no beards	Wide-brimmed hat similar to the **petasos** Peaked hat	Sandals Pointed toes		Crownlike headpieces
WOMEN	**Chiton** **Tebenna**	Archaic period: hair arranged in a single braid or in flowing tresses Post-Archaic hairstyles are similar to those of Greek women	Wide-brimmed hat, similar to the **petasos** **Tutulus**	Sandals Pointed toes	Necklaces, earrings, brooches, and fibulae	
CHILDREN (P. 80)	Small children naked in warm weather Boys: **tunics** Girls: **chitons** similar to those of the Greeks					

Roman Costume 500 B.C.–A.D. 400

	GARMENTS[A] (PP. 83–92)	UNDERGARMENTS (PP. 88–89)	FOOTWEAR (P. 90)	ACCESSORIES AND JEWELRY (P. 90)	COSMETICS (P. 90)	MILITARY (P. 92)	SPECIAL EVENTS (P. 93)
MEN	**Togas** for Roman male citizens Tunics, cloaks, and capes	**Subligar**	Sandals Laced boots for military use	Various white linen handkerchiefs Rings	Lavish use Perfume Use of public baths	Body armor; leather bands, metal plates **Abolla** **Sagum**	**Synthesis**
WOMEN	**Tunic** **Palla** **Stola** Garments designating social status: **stola**, **veil**, **vitta**, **tutulus**, **rincinium**, and **toga**	**Subligaria** **Strophium**	Sandals	Fans, handbags, and various white linen handkerchiefs Rings, necklaces, earrings, and diadems	Lavish use Perfume Use of public baths		Wedding costume: tunic, wool belt, **palla**, metal collar, and veil
CHILDREN	Swaddling **Bulla** (locket) wards off "evil eye" Children's dress similar to that of adults Special togas for freeborn children						

[A]For Roman headdress, *see* Illustrated Table 4.1, p. 91.

Relationship of Decorative and Fine Arts to Costume

Looking back at the "Decorative and Fine Arts Table" on page 16, choose one figure and describe how it relates to costume from this chapter.

Using the textbook and the "At a Glance" feature of Chapter Four of this study guide, can you sketch or describe the dress of the following people from Etruria or Rome?

1. Etruscan man wearing a **tebenna**

2. Etruscan woman in clothing showing Greek influences

3. Roman man wearing a **toga** of the imperial type

4. Free, married woman wearing an **under tunic**, a **stola**, and a **palla**

5. Roman woman dressed for an athletic competition

6. Roman boy wearing a **bulla** over a tunic

1. In what ways did Greek costume influence Etruscan styles? How did Etruscan costume influence Roman styles?

2. What features of Etruscan costume differentiate them from Greek costume?

3. Information about Etruscan costume comes from several sources. List the major ones, noting the problems those sources present.

4. Why is so much more known about Roman costume than about costume of the earlier periods?

5. The sources of evidence about Roman costume have some limitations. What are these?

6. Identify the components or decorative elements of Roman costume for men, for women, and for children that convey information about the SOCIAL STATUS of the wearer. Explain what these components would communicate to other Romans.

7. Using the comparison/contrast method, consider specific items of costume (for example, the Greek **himation** and the Roman **toga** or the Roman tunic and the Greek **chiton**) and identify the differences between Greek and Roman clothing. How do these differences reflect the different cultures?

8. Roman costume changed toward the close of the Imperial period. What were these changes, and how can they be seen as evidence of a decline of the power of the Empire?

NOTES

PART TWO The Middle Ages c. 300–1500

Read pages 99–106 and complete the following chart.

	TIME PERIOD	PRESENT-DAY COUNTRIES OCCUPYING THIS TERRITORY
CHAPTER 5		
CHAPTER 6		

After reading pages 99 to 103, can you answer the following questions?

1. Why were the early Middle Ages called "the Dark Ages"? (pp. 99–100)

2. What were the characteristics of feudal societies? (p. 100)

3. Why did the Europeans begin the Crusades? How long did the Crusades last? What kinds of products were brought to Europe as a result of the Crusades? (pp. 100–101)

4. How did Marco Polo's writings influence the development of trade with the Far East? (p. 101)

5. How do the authors define *fashion*, and what conditions must be present for fashion changes to occur? (pp. 102–103)

CHAPTER FIVE

The Early Middle Ages c. 300–1300

HISTORICAL SNAPSHOT

The Byzantine Empire (A.D. 339–1453) had as its capital Constantinople, a Greek city located at the entrance of the Black Sea. As a result of its command of major trade routes between the West and Central Asia, Russia, and the Far East, Constantinople was the metropolis of the Mediterranean economy. By the 6th century it controlled large areas around the Mediterranean (see Figure 5.1). Throughout its history Byzantium was at war with a series of enemies, including crusaders who sacked the city and displaced the emperor in 1204. In 1261, a Byzantine emperor retook Constantinople but the once-great Empire had vanished. Finally, in 1453, the Ottoman Turks captured the capital, destroying the Empire.

During the same time (300–1300) in Western Europe, the Roman Empire disintegrated. For centuries, Germanic tribes had been filtering into the Roman Empire in search of land. In some cases they intermarried with Romans, converted to Christianity, and established German kingdoms. After the fall of the Roman Empire, the most notable of these were the Merovingian Dynasty and the Carolingian Dynasty. A leader of the latter, Charlemagne (768–814), conquered Italy and was crowned emperor of the Romans, but his successes were not enough to unite the eastern and western sections of Europe, which had developed along separate lines since the end of the Roman Empire. Eventually, Carolingian rule collapsed under the impact of successive invasions, making way for feudal monarchies, the nations of the future.

In the 10th to the 13th centuries in Europe a "feudal system" of governance developed in which local rulers could call on their dependents for support in battles. Rulers in different regions had different titles and differing degrees of authority. When the Muslims gained control over the holy places of Christendom, the Catholic Church called upon the Western European nations to summon their warriors to a Crusade (1095) to regain control of the holy places. The last crusade ended in 1272.

MAJOR CONTENT AND THEMES OF THE EARLY MIDDLE AGES

As you read Chapter 5 (pp. 107–143), use the space provided to take notes about the chapter. Focus your attention on those areas that your instructor identifies as important. Return to Chapter 1, pages 3–10, and review the concept of *theme* as a unifying subject and idea related to dress. Try to identify examples of dress that relate to the themes identified in the summary on page 141. These notes will help you answer questions related to the key concepts and learning objectives, and later prepare for tests and projects.

Based on your reading of Chapter Five and your notes about the Early Middle Ages, can you answer the following questions?

1. Using Byzantine Period art to try to determine how people dressed during this period can pose problems. What are some of those challenges? (pp. 109–110)

2. What is **sericulture**, and how does it relate to costume? (p. 110)

3. What similarities and differences can you see in the dress of Romans and people living in the Byzantine Empire? (Chapter 4 and p. 114)

4. According to the textbook, who was likely to be responsible for the production of textiles in the Early Middle Ages in Europe? When and how did the organization of textile manufacturing change? (pp. 116, 124–125)

5. What are some early indications of fashion change, and why would the medieval towns and courts tend to encourage the wearing of fashionable dress? (pp. 124, 133)

6. How did the Crusades contribute to CROSS-CULTURAL INFLUENCES in costumes of the Early Middle Ages? (pp. 123, 141)

7. What fashions did one monk see as evidence of scandal and vice in the 12th century? (p. 133)

8. What was the influence of the styles of the Byzantine Period in Western Europe in the Early Middle Ages? Can you find examples in 20th-century fashions of ideas from the Early Middle Ages? (pp. 141–142)

Byzantine Costume A.D. 300–1450

	GARMENTS (PP. 110–113)	HAIR AND HEADDRESS (P. 113)	CLOAKS (P. 114)	FOOTWEAR (P. 114)	JEWELRY (P. 114)
MEN	Tunics of varying lengths; decoration depends on social position and time period Hose **Pallium**, or **lorum**	In the early period, men tend to be clean shaven In the later period, men tend to have beards Emperors wear jeweled crowns	Upper-class men wear **paludamentum** After 11th century, semicircular cloak for outdoor use **Tablion** Commoners wear a square cloak	Shoes, tied or buckled, with ornamentation Military wear Romanlike, open-toed boots	
WOMEN	Tunic and **palla** of Romans For the most part, tunics worn double-layered Veils	Hair usually covered Turbanlike hats, small caps, and so on Royal crowns are heavily jeweled with **diadems**	Empress wears **paludamentum** Commoners wear a simple square cloak	Shoes, tied or buckled, with ornamentation	Jewelry integral part of costume Empress wears wide, jeweled collars over the **paludamentum** Pins, earrings, bracelets, rings, and necklaces

Western Europe Fall of the Roman Empire to A.D. 900

	MEROVINGIAN PERIOD (PP. 117–119)	CAROLINGIAN PERIOD (PP. 117–119)	CLERICAL DRESS (PP. 119–120)
MEN	Tunics Byzantine influences for the wealthy and powerful Gartered hose Cloaks shaped like Greek **chlamys** King wears hair long; subjects wear hair short Boots and shoes	Similar to Merovingian dress, but tunics narrow at the body and widen at the skirt Men wear hair moderate length, below the ears Boots and shoes	Priests identifiable by **tonsure** (haircut) High-ranking priests wear distinctive ceremonial costume, including **amice**, **alb**, **chasuble**, **stole**, **pallium**, and **cope** Monks wear **cowls**
WOMEN	Loose-fitting shawls or draperies similar to the **palla**, over linen tunics Royal families import silk Jewels greatly influenced by Byzantine style	Shawls similar to the **palla**, draped over tunics Adult women drape shawls over their heads, cover their hair	Nuns wear veils Upon entering convent, women crop their hair

Anglo-Saxon and Norman Britain—Early Middle Ages

10TH AND 11TH CENTURIES	GARMENTS (PP. 126–128)	HAIR AND HEADDRESS (PP. 127–129)	FOOTWEAR AND LEG COVERINGS (PP. 128–129)
MEN	**Braies** of varying lengths	Young men are clean shaven	**Braies** or hose
	Double-layered tunics	Hoods	**Leg bandages**, or **gaiters**
	Tunic length, decoration indicate social class	**Phrygian bonnet**	Brightly colored socks
	Open mantles	Jewish men wear distinctive hats	Boots of varying heights
	Closed mantles		Shoes cut with slight point opposite big toe
			Clergy wear Byzantine-style slippers
WOMEN	**Chemise** underneath double-layered tunics	Young girls wear their hair loose	**Hose** tied into place around the knee
	Mantles, including fur-lined **winter mantles**	Married (and older) women cover their heads	**Clogs**
		The rich have silk or fine linen veils	

12TH CENTURY	GARMENTS (PP. 130, 132)	HAIR AND HEADDRESS (PP. 131–132)	FOOTWEAR (P. 131)
MEN	**Bliaut**	Hoods	Upper classes adopt long pointed shoe
	Bliaut gironé	Caps	
	Mantles	**Coif**	
	Sleeves more varied		
WOMEN	Lower-class costume unchanged	Upper classes arrange hair in two long plaits	No major changes
	Bliaut	Decorative ribbon	
	Bliaut gironé	**Barbettes**	
	Bliaut and tunic sleeves become longer and more varied	**Wimple** and veil	
	Chainse		
	Mantles		

Anglo-Saxon and Norman Britain—Early Middle Ages (cont'd.)

13TH CENTURY	GARMENTS (PP. 135, 137)	HAIR AND HEADDRESS (PP. 136–137)	FOOTWEAR AND LEG COVERINGS (PP. 137–138)
MEN	Emphasis on greater modesty at court **Magyar sleeve** Variations on the **surcote** include the **garnache, herigaut,** and **tabard** Use of slits, or **fitchets**	Moderate length, parted in the center Many men are beardless because of new closed military helmet **Coif** and hood **Cornette**, or **liripipe**	No major changes
WOMEN	**Chemise, cote, surcote, Magyar sleeve, mantle,** and cloak	Married and older women cover their heads with veils and hairnets Use of **barbettes, fillets,** and **wimples**	No major changes

10TH–13TH CENTURY	ACCESSORIES AND JEWELRY (P. 138)	COSMETICS (P. 138)	MILITARY (PP. 138–139)
MEN	Wallets, purses, and other carrying devices, usually suspended from belts Nobility and clergy wear gloves **Fermail** or **afiche**	Perfumes and ointments	Open and closed helmets, some with crests Chain **mail** **Hauberk, byrnie, chausses,** and **surcote** Change to plate armor begins end of 13th century
WOMEN		Perfumes, ointments, hair dyes, and face creams	

Relationship of Decorative and Fine Arts to Costume

Looking back at the "Decorative and Fine Arts Table" on page 104, choose one figure and describe how it relates to costume from this chapter.

Using the textbook and the "At a Glance" feature of Chapter Five of this study guide, can you sketch or describe the dress of the following people from the Early Middle Ages?

1. Man of the 11th century of the Byzantine Period

2. Byzantine woman of the 6th century

3. One of the garments that might be worn by Catholic priests

4. Man of the 12th century

5. Woman of the 13th century

6. Outdoor garment of the 13th or early 14th century

7. Soldier in the 12th century

1. Specific costume components from the Byzantine Period illustrate the notion that Byzantine costume reflects both the Roman and Oriental styles. How do these items show Roman influences? Oriental influences?

2. Who could wear the **paludamentum** and the **pallium** or **lorum** during the Byzantine Period? What might these restrictions indicate about the role of the empress in the Byzantine political system?

3. When and how was silk culture introduced to the Byzantine Empire? How did the production of silk contribute to the influence of Byzantine style in Western Europe?

4. How did the dress of the Merovingian and Carolingian rulers reflect both their differences from and their connections with the Byzantine Empire and the Christian church?

5. What aspects of clerical garb appear to be derived from Roman dress? How and why did monastic dress differ from clerical dress?

6. Beginning with the layer closest to the body and ending with the outermost garment, describe the garments that men and women would have worn in the 10th and 11th centuries. List the functions of each garment.

7. Beginning with the layer closest to the body and ending with the outermost garment, describe the garments men and women would have worn in the 12th and 13th centuries. List the functions of each garment.

8. Compare your answers to questions 6 and 7and describe how certain functions of these garments changed. In addition, explain how certain words related to the garments changed.

9. Chapter 1 of the text discussed some of clothing's functions. Identify some of the items of dress for men and for women in the periods included in Chapter 5 that might fulfill those functions. Try to find an example for each function.

10. How can the theme of POLITICAL CONFLICT be seen as a factor in the styles of the Byzantine and Early Medieval Periods?

NOTES

CHAPTER SIX

The Late Middle Ages c. 1300–1500

HISTORICAL SNAPSHOT

During the Late Middle Ages (1300–1500) in Europe, governments became more centralized, free peasants replaced serfs and paid rent to nobility, and cities and towns became an important source of tax revenue. The Black Death (plague) killed a third of Europe's population, making labor scarce, empowering the various guilds, and affording people of the lower classes the possibility of advancement. The growing merchant class was able to obtain and wear fashionable clothing, allowing for less-rigid class distinctions, and textiles became an important commodity available through trade. The noble courts were renowned for their luxury, extravagant costume, and lavish ceremony and entertainment.

MAJOR CONTENT AND THEMES OF THE LATE MIDDLE AGES

As you read Chapter 6 (pp. 145–173), use the space provided to take notes about the chapter. Focus your attention on those areas that your instructor identifies as important. Return to Chapter 1, pages 3–10, and review the concept of *theme* as a unifying subject and idea related to dress. Try to identify examples of dress that relate to the themes identified in the summary on page 170. These notes will help you answer questions related to the key concepts and learning objectives, and later prepare for tests and projects.

Based on your reading of Chapter Six and your notes about the Late Middle Ages, can you answer the following questions?

1. Medieval society can be seen as having consisted of three classes. What were they, and how did styles of dress differ from one class to another? (pp. 147–149)

2. Based on the description of fabrics and tailors (pp. 149–150), what kinds of skills and abilities were needed by people who produced and marketed textiles and clothing?

3. What sources does the costume historian have to study the dress of the Late Middle Ages? (pp. 150–151)

4. Carefully considering the changes in costume during the Late Middle Ages, explain the difference between the frequency of big modifications of silhouette and smaller details. What examples can you provide from the textbook that support your answer? (pp. 151–170)

5. What does the Italian writer Sacchetti see as the hazards of wearing fashionable clothes in the 14th century? (p. 159)

6. Why do you think the theme of GENDER DIFFERENCES appears to become more evident in the Late Middle Ages (Chapter 6 and p. 170) than in the Early Middle Ages? (Chapter 5)

7. Styles from the Late Middle Ages have been used by 20th-century fashion designers as inspiration. List some of these styles. (p. 172)

Late Middle Ages 14th Century

	GARMENTS (PP. 151–157)	HAIR AND HEADDRESS (PP. 154, 157–158)	FOOTWEAR (PP. 154–155, 158)	ACCESSORIES AND JEWELRY[A] (PP. 155, 158)	COSMETICS AND GROOMING (P. 158)	RITES OF PASSAGE (P. 168)
MEN	**Pourpoint**, or **doublet** or **gipon** **Set-in sleeves** **Cote-hardie** **Houppelande**, including **houppelande à mi-jambe** **Garnache**, **herigaut**, **houce**, **corset**, and other varied capes	Cut moderately short, below the ears **Coifs**, berets, caped hoods Second half of the century sees more fanciful headdress Clean shaven	Points at toes grow longer; most extreme forms worn by nobles Working-class men wear clogs in muddy weather	Belts with pouches Cuffed gloves		Long, black robes used for mourning
WOMEN	Dress for French royalty includes **gown**, **surcote**, **plastron**, and **skirt** **Houppelandes** reach their fullest development in the 1400s Capes, cloaks, and **herigauts** worn for warmth Fur linings common for winter: **lettice** for nobility; fox, otter, or **cony** for lower classes	Head coverings wide rather than high Narrow fillets worn over **fret** Hair hidden under a veil or held inside hair nets If visible, hair is plaited and either coiled around the ears or arranged parallel to the face Hoods or wide-brimmed hats for bad weather	Stockings end at knees and are tied in place Toes shorter than those on men's shoes	Gloves Necklaces, bracelets, earrings, rings, brooches, jeweled belts, and decorative buttons and clasps for mantles	Hair plucked around the face to achieve high forehead Hair dye and makeup used	Red popular for brides in some regions For brides, jewelry more important than specific clothing Widows wear wimples; black symbolizes mourning
CHILDREN (P. 168) 14TH AND 15TH CENTURIES	Loose **gowns** for little ones, after which children are dressed in the same manner as adults Gowns for royal children, made of rich fabrics, elaborately trimmed	Young girls go about with hair uncovered until marriage				Newborns wrapped in fur-trimmed mantles Baptismal linen used

[A]For late-Middle-Ages accessories, see Illustrated Table 6.1, p. 156.

	GARMENTS (PP. 158–161, 163–164)	HAIR AND HEADDRESS[A] (PP. 161, 164)	FOOTWEAR (PP. 161–162, 168)	ACCESSORIES (PP. 162, 168)	SPECIALIZED OCCUPATIONS IN THE MIDDLE AGES (PP. 168–170)
MEN	**Doublet** placed over the undershirt, beneath the jacket **Hose** covering lower part of body, exposed **Codpiece** **Houppelandes** (fur-lined in winter) of many lengths Open and closed cuff sleeve styles **Cote-hardie** replaced by alternative **jacket** style Cloaks or full capes chief outdoor garment for working men	**Bowl crop** Neck shaved below cut hair After midcentury, **pageboy** style Variety of head coverings **Coif** gradually disappears, except in the dress of clergy and professions such as medicine	Lower-class men wear stockings Pointed foot coverings; very long points are stuffed **Pattens** Long, riding-style boots become popular for general wear	Jeweled collars, daggers, pouches, gloves, and decorative belts In the first half of the 1400s, a man's belt is one of his most important possessions	Some out-of-date fashions become traditional for particular professions During the 1400s, students retain the cote and surcote after it has been abandoned for general wear Military dress includes **coat of plates**, **gambeson**, **haubergeon**, and rounded helmets with hinged visors
WOMEN	Women tend to wear linen undergarments and one or two layers of outer garments **Smock** Long **houppelandes**, belted above waistline **Rocs**, or **frocks** (loose-fitting gowns) **Bagpipe sleeves**, tubular sleeves, hanging sleeves, and other sleeve shapes **Gown**, or **cote**, of soft, gathered fullness; edges of V-shaped neckline turned back into **revers**, with modesty piece worn underneath Long **skirts**	Unmarried girls, brides, and queens at their coronation can show their hair Hair plucked around the face to achieve high forehead **Hennin** Variety of headdress styles; sheer veils draped over headdresses	Stockings end at the knee, tie around the leg Shoes fit the foot closely Wooden **pattens** worn in bad weather	Jewelry, gloves, purses, and girdles (belts) With lower necklines, necklaces gain importance	

[A]For 15th-century headdress, see Illustrated Table 6.2, p. 167.

Relationship of Decorative and Fine Arts to Costume

Looking back at the "Decorative and Fine Arts Table" on page 104, choose one figure and describe how it relates to costume from this chapter.

Using the textbook and the "At a Glance" feature of Chapter Six of this study guide, can you sketch or describe the dress of the following people from the Late Middle Ages?

1. Working man of the period 1340–1400

2. French queen of the late 1300s

3. Young, upper-class man of the period 1450–1500

4. Unmarried girl of about 1400

5. Woman of the second half of the 15th century

6. Knight dressed for battle in the 15th century

1. Increasing international trade and interchange of ideas were reflected in some aspects of costume in the 14th and 15th centuries. List some examples of this two-way influence.

2. What are the major sources of information about costume in the 14th and 15th centuries? Why is more information available to the costume historian for these periods than for the earlier centuries of the Middle Ages? What are the strengths and weaknesses of the available information?

3. The names for items of costume are often related to their function, their appearance, or some other characteristic. List some items from the 14th and 15th centuries that have such names, and describe how they relate to function, appearance, or some other characteristic.

4. The theme of SOCIAL CLASS or rank is reflected in some individual costume items or elements of costume in the 14th and 15th centuries. What examples of this can you find in the textbook? Identify the rank or class status that each item indicated.

5. Identify and describe the various stages in the dress of children from birth to adulthood.

6. Dress can serve as a form of non-verbal communication. What kind of garments or grooming might a medieval man or woman use to communicate the following: widowhood, student status, readiness for war, and membership in the household of a particular noble?

7. Thorsten Veblen, an economist, spoke of dress as a way of showing status through **conspicuous consumption** (i.e., wearing something that is obviously costly) and through **conspicuous leisure** (wearing something that shows that a person does not need to do hard work). What are some examples of clothing of the 14th and 15th centuries that would demonstrate conspicuous consumption? Conspicuous leisure?

NOTES

PART THREE

The Renaissance c. 1400–1600

Read pages 175–180 and complete the following chart.

	TIME PERIOD	PRESENT DAY COUNTRIES OCCUPYING THIS TERRITORY
CHAPTER 7		
CHAPTER 8		

After reading pages 175 to 177, can you answer the following questions?

1. What aspects of Italian history and geography contributed to the development of the Renaissance in Italy? (175–176)

2. In what ways is the Renaissance still influential in modern life? (175–177)

CHAPTER SEVEN

The Italian Renaissance c. 1400–1600

HISTORICAL SNAPSHOT

The Renaissance (1400–1600) can be viewed as a time of transition from the medieval to a modern view of man and the world. At the time of the Renaissance, the word *Italy* referred not to a country but to a geographic area made up of a number of small city-states ruled by princes. The population was roughly divided among the aristocracy, the merchant class, artisans and artists, town laborers, and the peasants of the countryside. Although men of aristocratic families made up the ruling class in most cities, in some places ruling families came from a merchant background, and most large businesses were in some way related to the textile industry, weaving, dyeing, finishing, or trading cloth. Wool and silk were the primary fabrics used in Italy, and many of the fabrics of the day utilized patterns and decorative motifs that reflected close trading contacts between Italy and the Far East.

It is worth noting that Renaissance patrons supported artists who are still considered among the greatest of Western Civilization, and their art provides an extensive record of the clothing worn during the Italian Renaissance.

MAJOR CONTENT AND THEMES OF THE ITALIAN RENAISSANCE

As you read Chapter Seven (pp. 175–201), use the space provided to take notes about the chapter. Focus your attention on those areas that your instructor identifies as important. Return to Chapter 1, pages 3–10, and review the concept of *theme* as a unifying subject and idea related to dress. Try to identify examples of dress that relate to the themes identified in the summary on page 198. These notes will help you answer questions related to the key concepts and learning objectives, and later prepare for tests and projects.

Based on your reading of Chapter Seven and your notes about the major themes of the Italian Renaissance, can you answer the following questions?

1. From what social class did the rulers of most Italian city-states come? In what occupation did people tend to be most wealthy? (pp. 182–183)

2. In addition to the groups identified in Question 1, who else tried to follow fashion (according to the textbook)? List the types of historical sources mentioned as providing evidence for this conclusion. (p. 183)

3. What kinds of textiles were used for clothing during this period? Who made clothing from these textiles? (pp. 183–184)

4. The theme of CROSS-CULTURAL INFLUENCES was particularly important in Italian Renaissance styles. Describe how styles in Italy were influenced by other cultures. (pp. 184, 198)

5. What items of dress worn by women of Venice in Italy were so remarkable that they were remarked upon by visitors from other countries? (p. 196)

6. What sources provide evidence about the fashions of the Italian Renaissance? (p. 184)

7. In what areas can Italian Renaissance costume be seen as having an influence during the past 100 years? (p. 200)

The Italian Renaissance 1450–1500

	GARMENTS[A] (PP. 187–192)	HAIR AND HEADDRESS (PP. 189, 192)	FOOTWEAR (PP. 189, 192)	JEWELRY (P. 192)
MEN	**Camicia** Shirts worn visible at the openings of outermost garments; sleeves and body cut in one piece, with gussets **Doublets** (and **jackets**) with distinctive necklines Hose made from woven fabrics; laces untied for physical activity Decorative hanging sleeves Full-length ceremonial robes Fur-trimmed open and closed capes for warmth	Medium to longer lengths; older men cut their hair shorter Men are generally clean shaven Variety of hat styles, including turbanlike styles, pillbox styles, and hats with soft crowns and upturned brims or round crowns and narrow brims	Pointed toes begin to round off by the end of the century Most popular footwear: leather-soled footed hose Boots, worn in bad weather or for riding, have turned-down cuffs, end mid-calf	
WOMEN	Chemise (**camicia**) worn as an undergarment beneath a dress, with a second overdress on top Lavish use of opulent fabric for upper-class women At mid-century, rounded necklines, cut high; lower necklines by end of century Sleeve styles similar to men's Open and closed **mantles,** or capes	Elaborate arrangements of buns, braids, loops, and curls; very different from style of northern European women (who cover their heads) "Token" head covers	Rarely seen in paintings, women's shoes appear be cut along the same lines as those of men	Necklaces, earrings, brooches, and many interesting hair ornaments **Ferroniere**

16th Century

	GARMENTS (PP. 192–195)	HAIR AND HEADDRESS (PP. 193, 195)	VENETIAN COSTUME (PP. 195–197)
MEN	French and Spanish influence by mid-century **Camicia** with embroidered necklines Narrow silhouettes Large **codpieces,** c. 1500 **Codpieces** disappear by latter part of the century	Men begin to wear beards again	Anatomical waistlines Nobility wear special, distinctive costumes
WOMEN	**Camicia** sometimes cut high Silhouettes of dresses grow wider and fuller Spanish-influenced dresses with V-shaped waists gain popularity as the century progresses	**Turbans**	Distinctly high **chopines** Hair arranged at the front in little twin "horns" Hair bleached to light blond shades Underdrawers
CHILDREN (P. 197)	Once out of swaddling clothes, adultlike dress		

[A]For Italian Renaissance accessories, see Illustrated Table 7.1, p. 194.

Relationship of Decorative and Fine Arts to Costume

Looking back at the "Decorative and Fine Arts Table" on page 178, choose one figure and describe how it relates to costume from this chapter.

Using the textbook and the "At a Glance" feature of Chapter Seven of this study guide, can you sketch or describe the dress of the following people from the Renaissance?

1. Italian woman of about 1400–1450 wearing a hat with a possible Middle Eastern influence

2. Italian workman of about 1450–1500

3. Upper-class Italian woman of 1450–1500

4. Upper-class Italian man of the 16th century

5. Upper-class woman of the 16th century whose **camecia** can be seen at the neckline and sleeve edges

6. Venetian woman of the last half of the 16th century

1. Explain how Italian Renaissance costumes, especially in cities like Florence, were influenced by the business interests of local merchants.

2. Italian dress also reflected cross-cultural influences from the Middle East. List some specific Middle Eastern influences.

3. What are the major sources of information about Italian Renaissance costume practices? What are the strengths and weaknesses of these sources?

4. Describe a few similarities and differences between costume in Italy and costume in Northern Europe in the second half of the 15th century. Describe a few similarities and differences in those same areas in the 16th century.

5. What were some unique aspects of Venetian costume in the 15th and 16th centuries?

6. What foreign elements influenced Italian costume in the 16th century? Why did foreign influences come to dominate? What were some of these influences?

CHAPTER EIGHT

The Northern Renaissance c. 1500–1600

HISTORICAL SNAPSHOT

The spirit of the Renaissance in the arts and in philosophy gradually moved to northern Europe. Along with changes in arts and letters came changes in religious attitudes, which culminated in the Protestant Reformation. This revolution against the Roman Catholic Church started in the German states and spread throughout the German Holy Roman Empire, which included the Hapsburg Territories, the Low Countries, and Spain—all of which came under the control of one man, Emperor Charles V.

Spain dominated Europe throughout the early part of the century because of Charles V's political interests and the wealth acquired through trade in goods from the Americas. When Charles V abdicated the throne and divided the Empire between his son and his brother, the Holy Roman Empire was effectively ended (although it nominally existed until 1806) and Spain's political influence gradually began to wane.

Religious tensions were common across Europe. In England, Henry VIII split with the Church of Rome over its refusal to let him divorce his Spanish queen, Katharine of Aragon, and established a national Church of England. After a brief return to the Roman Church, Henry's daughter, Elizabeth, resolved the direction of the Church of England and instituted the basis for the standard of English Protestantism. In France, Protestant Bourbon Henry IV converted to Roman Catholicism and soothed religious problems by issuing the Edict of Nantes, guaranteeing rights to all Protestants.

Throughout this period, increased travel and printed books brought greater cross-cultural influences to dress in Europe, and wealth from trade and conquests made courts a center for the display of changing fashions.

MAJOR CONTENT AND THEMES OF THE NORTHERN RENAISSANCE

As you read Chapter 8 (pp. 203–227), use the space provided to take notes about the chapter. Focus your attention on those areas that your instructor identifies as important. Return to Chapter 1, pages 3–10, and review the concept of theme as a unifying subject and idea related to dress. Try to identify examples of dress that relate to the themes identified in the summary on page 226. These notes will help you answer questions related to the key concepts and learning objectives, and later prepare for tests and projects.

Based on your reading of Chapter Eight and your notes about the major themes of the Northern Renaissance, can you answer the following questions?

1. According to the textbook, what factors helped to spread new fashion information in Europe during the 16th century? (p. 206)

2. How did the Middle East continue to influence European fashion? (pp. 206–207)

3. When did hand knitting apparently begin in Europe? When and where was mechanized knitting introduced? (p. 207)

4. What important decorative techniques were used in the 16th century to ornament clothing? What are a few examples of the clothing they were used to decorate? (pp. 207–208, 212–223)

5. List some sources that can be used to study costume of the 16th century. (p. 208)

6. What can you learn about ruffs and how they were worn from the writings of a Puritan who objected to these garments? (p. 214)

7. How did the development of a more international style in fashion in the 16th century reflect the themes of COMMUNICATION and of CROSS-CULTURAL INFLUENCES? (pp. 224, 226)

8. What elements of 16th-century dress does the textbook mention as surviving in later periods? (p. 226)

Northern Renaissance: 16th Century

	GARMENTS (PP. 208–220)	HAIR AND HEADDRESS (PP. 220–222)	FOOTWEAR (PP. 222–223)	JEWELRY AND ACCESSORIES (P. 223)[A]	COSMETICS (P. 223)
MEN					
1500–1515 (PP. 208–210)	Linen shirts with embroidered necklines and long, **raglan sleeves** **Doublets** and hose laced together Filler, or **stomacher**, of contrasting colors **Jerkin**, or **jacket** **Bases** **Gowns** are long garments with huge funnel-shaped sleeves; younger men wear shorter **gowns**	Hair cut straight across the back, length ranges from below the ear to the shoulder Hats placed over skull caps or hairnets Early in the century, fashionable hat styles include the **French bonnet**: pillbox-like shape, with a turned-up brim Many hats decorated with feathers, jewels, and braids After 1530, beards become fashionable, mustaches popular After midcentury, high-crowned hats with stiff outlines **Copotain** popular	Men's styles more exaggerated than women's Square-toed shapes expand as the period progresses In the latter half of the century, wide shoes, **duckbills**, mules, and high heels popular	Lavish jewelry for royals and wealthy men during the first half of the century Gold neck chains, brooches, rings, jeweled collars, and so on Purses carried by men and women, often suspended by belts In second half of the century: use of smaller, more restrained jewelry pieces	
1515–1550 (PP. 210–211)	Puffier silhouettes Decorative **slashings**, or **panes** **Upper stocks** and **nether stocks**; upper stocks take on appearance of separate garment Padded **codpieces** Wider **gowns**				
1550–1600 (PP. 211–213)	Decreased shoulder width, and men no longer appear in short jackets or longer skirted jackets and hose **Trunk hose** and separate breeches **Codpieces** gradually go out of style **Ruffs** Doublet necks cut high **Peascod belly** **Galligaskins**, or **slops** **Culots** Doublets padded with **bombast** **Canions**				

[A]For Northern Renaissance accessories, see Illustrated Table 8.1, p. 221.

Northern Renaissance: 16th Century (cont'd.)

		GARMENTS (PP. 208–220)	HAIR AND HEADDRESS (PP. 220–222)	FOOTWEAR (PP. 222–223)	JEWELRY AND ACCESSORIES (P. 223)[A]	COSMETICS (P. 223)
WOMEN	**1500–1530 (P. 215)**	Undergarments begin taking on "shaping" role **Corsets** **Busks** made from whalebone **Chemise, gowns** with fitted bodices Skirts are long and full, and women wear single- or two-layer dresses Square necklines Trains have decorative underlining Except for ceremonial occasions, long, full-length cloaks worn outdoors	Married and adult women continue to cover their hair **Coifs** Decorative overcaps sometimes placed over **coif**, some trimmed with jewels or netting Many hats decorated with feathers	Styles similar to men's Styles worn only by women include low-cut slippers with a strap across the ankle and **chopines** In the latter half of the century, wide shoes, **duckbills**, mules, and high heels popular	Lavish jewelry; jeweled decorations applied to almost any part of the costume Gold neck chains, pendants, brooches, rings, jeweled collars, and so on Jeweled belts with purse cords and purses	Made from dangerous chemicals (e.g., mercurial salts) Red coloring applied to lips and cheeks Perfumes Puritans rally against these "evil practices" in the latter part of the century
	GERMANY: 1530–1575 (PP. 215–216)	Elaborate bodices **Chemise**-filled necklines Close-fitting sleeves	Hair held in a net, over which is placed a wide-brimmed hat trimmed with plumes More hair becomes visible in the last two-thirds of the century		Fans, handkerchiefs, and gloves popular accessories throughout the century	
	OTHER NORTHERN EUROPEAN COUNTRIES: 1530–1575 (PP. 216-218)	Hourglass silhouette Bodices and overskirts sewn together; **petticoat** sometimes visible through opening in skirt Stiffly rigid skirt styles Variety of sleeve styles **Aiguillettes** (fasteners) **Verdugale** **Spanish farthingale** **Ropa**	Local differences in hairstyles arise Hair dressed high, and decorations added Popular hats at the end of the century are smaller, with high crowns and narrow brims		Masks worn outdoors to protect against sun Gold chains worn, along with a wide "dog collar" Spider-shaped pins to hold ruffs **Aiguilletes** Earrings gain popularity as more hair becomes visible	
	1575–1600 (PP. 219–220)	Wider skirt shape **Bum rolls** **Wheel** or **drum** or **French farthingale** Ruffs grow to enormous widths, supported by **supportasse** **Medici collars** **Conch**, or **conque**	Englishwomen copy Elizabeth's red hair		**Ferronieres**, in France	
CHILDREN		Children's dress similar to that of adults; some male children dress in skirts until age 4–5; royal children wear elaborate, costly silks made into heavy velvets and brocades				

[A]For Northern Renaissance accessories, see Illustrated Table 8.1, p. 221.

Relationship of Decorative and Fine Arts to Costume

Looking back at the "Decorative and Fine Arts Table" on page 178, choose one figure and describe how it relates to costume from this chapter.

Using the textbook and the "At a Glance" feature of Chapter Eight of this study guide, can you sketch or describe the dress of the following people from the Northern Renaissance?

1. Upper-class German woman of the early 16th century

2. Henry VIII of England

3. Woman of the third decade of the 1500s

4. Upper-class woman wearing the farthingale dress style

5. Upper-class or royal child under the age of 5

1. Why were Spanish influences on costume so strong in the 16th century?

2. Items of dress are often named for their appearance or for the function or location of the item. What might be the origins of stomacher, bases, peascod belly, ruff, bum roll, duck-bill, and points?

3. What important 16th-centrury technological advancement permanently changed the way stockings were made?

4. Describe how the silhouette of men's costume changed during the 16th century. What techniques were used to provide support for these shapes?

5. Describe how the silhouette of women's costume changed during the 16th century. What techniques were used to provide support for these shapes?

6. What were the differences, if any, between the clothing of children and that of adults in the 16th century?

NOTES

Read pages 229–236 and complete the following chart.

	TIME PERIOD	PRESENT DAY COUNTRIES OCCUPYING THIS TERRITORY
CHAPTER 9		
CHAPTER 10		

After reading pages 229 to 233, can you answer the following questions?

1. During the 17th century, which countries became the focus of increased trade with the Far East? (pp. 230–231)

2. What types of textiles were brought to Europe as a result of Eastern trade? (pp. 231–232)

3. What is the meaning of the term *Industrial Revolution*? What inventions associated with the Industrial Revolution contributed to the transformation of the clothing manufacturing industry? (p. 232)

4. What are some of the ways that information about new fashions was communicated visually during the time period covered in Part Four? (pp. 232–233)

CHAPTER NINE

The Seventeenth Century 1600–1700

HISTORICAL SNAPSHOT

The major powers in 17th-century Europe were France, England, and Spain. Italy remained divided into small political units dominated by other countries. Holland had become independent of Spain, and the German princes, technically within the Holy Roman Empire, were sovereign powers. Colonial enterprises and trade continued to be a major source of revenue for the European powers. In the arts, Renaissance styles gave way to Mannerism and finally to the Baroque styles.

MAJOR CONTENT AND THEMES OF THE 17TH CENTURY

As you read Chapter Nine (pp. 237–263), use the space provided to take notes about the chapter. Focus your attention on those areas that your instructor identifies as important. Return to Chapter 1, pages 3–10, and review the concept of *theme* as a unifying subject and idea related to dress. Try to identify examples of dress that relate to the themes identified in the summary on page 260. These notes will help you answer questions related to the key concepts and learning objectives, and later prepare for tests and projects.

Based on your reading of Chapter Nine and your notes about the major themes of the 17th century, can you answer the following questions?

1. The dress of Puritans and the dress of those at the Spanish court differed from fashionable dress elsewhere in Europe. What were a few of these differences? (pp. 241–242)

2. What was the difference between a tailor and a seamstress in the early 17th century? What changes that took place later in the 17th century affected their work? (p. 243)

3. What problems might a costume historian encounter when using depictions of costume of the 17th century to determine what people wore? (pp. 243–244)

4. What is the garment that some fashion historians consider to be the forerunner of a man's three-piece suit? Where was it worn and by whom? How does it relate to the theme of CROSS-CULTURAL INFLUENCES? (pp. 248, 249)

5. One historian, Aries, suggests that it was in the 17th century that a costume specifically for children was first used. What was this costume and what was its origin? (pp. 258–259)

6. Did any elements of 17th-century styles reappear in later fashions? If so, give an example. (p. 262)

17th Century

		GARMENTS	HAIR AND HEADDRESSES	FOOTWEAR	ACCESSORIES AND JEWELRY FOR MEN AND WOMEN[A] (PP. 256–258)	COSMETICS AND GROOMING (P. 258)
MEN	1625–1650 (PP. 244–247)	Linen shirts, cut full, flat collared, become more integral part of the whole costume Doublets worn over shirts and laced to breeches High waistlines For outdoors, capes and cloaks with wide collars **Balagny cloaks, cassocks,** or **casaques**	Hair worn long and curling Beards worn to a point; mustaches are large and curled **"Love lock"**	Shoes and boots have high heels and **straight soles** (prior to high heels, shoes were shaped for right or left feet) **Slap soles** Boots extend to the knee, where they meet breeches **Latchets** Knee-length hose or stockings worn under shoes or boots	Scented gloves Handkerchiefs Purses Fans, made of feathers or of the folding type Women carry muffs made of silk, velvet, satin, fur, or fur-trimmed fabrics Women wear face masks	Women and some men use cosmetics Perfume is applied to person and clothing Lead combs used to darken eyebrows; paint and powder tint the face **Patches** cover blemishes Night masks **Plumpers**
	1650–1680 (PP. 247–248)	Shirts continue to become more visible and important Doublets shortened **Petticoat breeches,** or **rhinegraves; vests** introduced (possible oriental antecedents); combination of vest, long coat, narrow breeches is the prototype of the three-piece suit Cloaks and capes	Some men shave their heads and wear long curling wigs; others decorate their natural hair in curling style "Cavaliers" wear wide-brimmed, low-crowned, feathered hat Puritans wear high-crowned, small-brimmed **copotains** Men wear hats indoors and out and in church	Elaborate rosette, ribbon, and buckle trimmings Red-heeled and soled shoes popular in France and England **Galosh**	Aprons Jewelry includes chains, pendants, lockets, rings, and earrings Mirrors and **pomanders**	
	1680–1710 (P. 250)	Shirts little changed **Cravats** replace collars Knee-length coats replace doublets; **surtouts,** or **justacorps,** and **cassocks** Vest or **waistcoat,** shorter and less full than outer coats Breeches end at knees	Larger wigs; hair built up on top of the head Hats often superfluous, given hair size, and carried rather than worn **Tricorne**	Styles similar to those from earlier centuries Shoe buckles are made to transfer from one shoe to another **Jack boots**		

[A]For 17th-century accessories, see Table 9.1, p. 252.

17th Century (cont'd.)

		GARMENTS	HAIR AND HEADDRESSES	FOOTWEAR	ACCESSORIES AND JEWELRY FOR MEN AND WOMEN[A] (PP. 256–258)	COSMETICS AND GROOMING (P. 258)
WOMEN	**1630–1660 (PP. 251–254)**	White linen chemise undergarment Gowns made with bodices and skirts seamed at waist; outer layer worn beneath an under-bodice Skirts are separate garments, worn under gowns **Modeste** **Secret** Jackets and skirts can be worn instead of gowns Full sleeves **Virago sleeves** Low necklines; various styles Capes worn out-of-doors	Hair parted at the ears and drawn into a roll or **chignon** at back; front hair arranged in curls around the face Women both wear hats and go bareheaded; "cavalier-style" hats and copotains are worn Squares of fabric worn under the chin Hoods	Similar in shape to men's Clogs with toe caps, instep straps, no heels, and wooden soles used for bad weather	Scented gloves Handkerchiefs Purses Fans, made of feathers or of the folding type Women carry muffs made of silk, velvet, satin, fur, or fur-trimmed fabrics Women wear face masks Aprons Jewelry includes chains, pendants, lockets, rings, and earrings Mirrors and **pomanders**	Women and some men use cosmetics Perfume is applied to person and clothing Lead combs used to darken eyebrows; paint and powder tint the face **Patches** cover blemishes Night masks **Plumpers**
	1660–1680 (PP. 254–255)	Chemises and under-petticoats worn as undergarments Silhouettes change; bodices lengthen and get narrower, with extended V-shape at front Brightly colored fabrics Low, wide, oval- shaped necks edged by **whisks** Ruffles down the front, or lines of jeweled decorations and braids placed on top of seam construction lines	Some men shave their heads and wear long curling wigs; others decorate their natural hair in curling style "Cavaliers" wear wide-brimmed, low-crowned, feathered hat Puritans wear high-crowned, small-brimmed **copotains** Men wear hats indoors and out and in church	Elaborate rosette, ribbon, and buckle trimmings Red-heeled and soled shoes popular in France and England **Galosh**		
	1680–1700 (PP. 255–256)	No major changes in undergarments Styles of gowns evolve; necklines reveal less bosom, are more square Corsets, heavily decorated, visible at front of bodice Separate **stomachers** Heavy skirts require supports New skirt construction: bodices and skirts cut in length, shoulder to hem **Mantua, or manteau** For outdoors, capes, long scarves, and **lappets** are all worn	Hair is built high on top of the head, with long curling locks at backs and sides **Fontange**, or **commode**	Shoes become more pointed, heels become higher and narrower Brocades and decorative leathers **Pantofles** Stockings knitted by machine and hand, with knitted or embroidered decorations		
CHILDREN (PP. 258–260)		Infant costume components: swaddling bands, bibs, caps (**biggins**), shirts, mittens, sleeves, and **tailclouts**, or **nappies** Infants swaddled for the first 2 or 3 months; then, bands removed and **stays**, **staybands**, or **rollers** tied tightly around the body Sequence of boy's costume: swaddling clothes, skirt, robe, and apron (the robe is a distinctive item of clothing for boys); by age 3 or 4 the boy dons the long robe, an d by 6 or 7 he is dressed in adult male styles Terms related to 17th-century children's costume also include **leading strings**, **ribbons of childhood**, **carrying frocks**, **going frock**, **pinafore**, **muckinder**, and **pudding**				

[A]For 17th-century accessories, see Table 9.1, p. 252.

Relationship of Decorative and Fine Arts to Costume

Looking back at the "Decorative and Fine Arts Table" on page 234, choose one figure and describe how it relates to costume from this chapter.

Using the textbook and the "At a Glance" feature of Chapter Nine of this study guide, can you sketch or describe the dress of the following people from the 17th century?

1. Gentleman of about 1625–1650

2. Woman of the period when the artist Peter Paul Rubens was active

3. Man wearing **rhinegraves** or **petticoat breeches**, of about 1650–1680

4. Woman wearing a **mantua** and a **fontange**

5. Newborn infant

FINAL REVIEW QUESTIONS

1. What are some of the specific ways that royalty directly influenced fashions in dress during the 17th century?

2. How did the dress of Spanish upper-class men and women differ from the dress of upper-class men and women in other European countries? What seems to have been the basis for these differences?

3. How did the clothing of members of the Puritan and Royalist factions in the English Civil War differ? What seems to have been the basis for these differences?

4. Describe the evolution of style in men's breeches from the beginning to the end of the 17th century.

5. What are some specific examples of CROSS-CULTURAL INFLUENCES from non-Western dress on Western dress in the 17th century?

6. The origins of the modern three-piece suit for men are said to be found in the 17th century. What are these origins?

7. List similarities and differences between children's dress and adult's dress of the 17th century.

NOTES

CHAPTER TEN

The Eighteenth Century 1700–1790

HISTORICAL SNAPSHOT

Despite costly wars and a mounting fiscal crisis, France dominated the culture of Western Europe throughout the first half of the 18th century. However, the lavish court lifestyle contrasted sharply with the lives of ordinary citizens, and by the second half of the century, Frenchmen who wanted reform were encouraged not only by the success of the American Revolution, but also by English influence, particularly in the areas of government and civil rights. In 1789, the bankruptcy of the French government forced the calling of the Estates General, which declared itself a National Assembly, abolished feudalism, and began to write a constitution. In 1793, the king and queen of France were executed and the old regime was abolished.

Georgian England was ruled by the Hanoverian kings, who were of German extraction. The organization of society was less court-centered in England than in France, and both the upper class and the growing middle class kept up with fashion, vacationed at spas, and took part in various forms of popular entertainment where they might observe the latest fashions.

During this period, the Baroque style gave way to the more curvilinear forms of the Rococo, which were replaced in the last half of the century by a revival of Classical influences in the Neoclassical Period. Also during this period, international trade brought Asian influences to Europe, and advances in textile technology foreshadowed the Industrial Revolution.

MAJOR CONTENT AND THEMES OF THE 18TH CENTURY

As you read Chapter Ten (pp. 265–293), use the space provided to take notes about the chapter. Focus your attention on those areas that your instructor identifies as important. Return to Chapter 1, pages 3–10, and review the concept of *theme* as a unifying subject and idea related to dress. Try to identify examples of dress that relate to the themes identified in the summary on page 292. These notes will help you answer questions related to the key concepts and learning objectives, and later prepare for tests and projects.

Based on your reading of Chapter Ten and your notes about the major themes of the 18th Century, can you answer the following questions?

1. A number of French women were important at different times during the 1700s. Who were the following women and why was each important to fashion and history? (p. 267)
   a. Madame Pompadour

   b. Queen Marie Antoinette

2. If you were transported back to 18th-century England, why might you have difficulty understanding what people were talking about when they discussed clothes? (pp. 268–269)

3. According to the text, what was a "breeches club" and how did it help people obtain clothing? (pp. 269–270)

4. Why is it easier to research 18th-century dress than that of earlier periods? What art traditions in portraiture make it difficult to determine what people actually wore? (p. 270)

5. How did the philosopher Jean-Jacques Rousseau influence children's dress in the second half of the 18th century? What were some of his recommendations? (pp. 288–289)

6. Who is Thorstein Veblen? How does his theory relate to the theme of ECONOMICS in fashion? (p. 290)

7. Some of the names given to 18th-century fashions are still in use today. What are a few of these terms, and what do they mean? (p. 292)

18th Century

	GARMENTS (PP. 271–276, 279–284)	HAIR AND HEADDRESS[A] (PP. 276, 281, 282, 244)	FOOTWEAR (PP. 276, 284)	ACCESSORIES AND JEWELRY[B] (PP. 277, 285–287)	COSMETICS AND GROOMING (PP. 277, 287)	ACTIVE SPORTS (P. 287)
MEN	Major elements include underdrawers, shirt, waistcoat, an outer coat, knee-length breeches, hose, and shoes **Drawers** worn beneath breeches, next to the skin, made of cotton or wool First half of the century: collars gather to neckband, concealed by cloths or cravats **Steinkirk** **Boot cuffs** Waistcoats end close to knee; made with or without sleeves **Frock coats** **Ditto suit** Mid-century: fullness of coats decreases; silhouette narrows; waistcoats are sleeveless and shorter, both single- and double-breasted; cravats replaced by **stocks** Second half of the century: **surtouts,** or greatcoats, end below the knee, coat sleeves are cuffed **Indian gowns**, or **banyans**	Various styles of wigs; favored styles shift throughout century; hats become less important **"Full-bottomed" wigs** **Toupee**, or **foretop** Hair dressed higher after 1750 and wider in the 1780s Popular styles include **queues** and **club wigs**, or **catogans** Hats include **chapeau bras**, **tricornes**, and **bicornes**	Stockings end above the knee Shoes become rounder, with high square heels and large square tongues Decorative buckles used Red heels favored for court dress **Splatterdashers,** or **spats** Various boots for riding, traveling, hunting, and military	Muffs, walking sticks, watches, pocketbooks, and decorative snuff boxes	Powder and perfume	No special riding or hunting costumes Special bathing costume

[A]For 18th-century hairstyles and headdress, *see* Illustrated Table 10.2, p. 286.

[B]For 18th-century accessories, *see* Illustrated Table 10.1, p. 278.

18th Century (cont'd.)

		GARMENTS (PP. 271–276, 279–284)	HAIR AND HEADDRESS[A] (PP. 276, 281, 282, 244)	FOOTWEAR (PP. 276, 284)	ACCESSORIES AND JEWELRY[B] (PP. 277, 285–287)	COSMETICS AND GROOMING (PP. 277, 287)	ACTIVE SPORTS (P. 287)
WOMEN	**1715–1730**	Variety of undergarments determine costume shape **Paniers** **Hoops** (early versions made of whalebone) Extreme width of costumes make it necessary to enter rooms sideways Drawers not yet universally worn; women wear chemises, under petticoats and hoops Under petticoats made of **cambric, dimity, flannel,** or **calico** Corsets, or **stays** **Gowns** loose or fitted **Sacque,** or **robe battante** or **robe volante** or **innocente** **Pet-en-lair** **Mantua**-style gown	**Fontange** out of style by c. 1710 Waved loosely around face, tied in bun at back Hair powdered on formal occasions Hats worn indoors and out; women wear **pinners** or **mob caps** indoors	Knee-length stockings held in place by garters Shoes have pointed toes, high heels, tongues, and **latchets** **Mules** **Clogs** or **pattens**	Gloves, mittens, and muffs Pockets are bags sewn onto ribbon and tied around the waist Folding fans, parasols, and masks Jewelry includes necklaces, earrings, watches worn from the neck, jeweled hair pins and ornaments, and ornamental buckles	Lips, cheeks, fingernails colored red with rouge **"Wash balls"**	Riding costume adapted from men's styles Special riding hats Special bathing costume
	1730–1760	Loose **sacque** replaced by **robe à la Française** and **robe à l'Anglaise** Open bodices and skirts displaying decorative stomachers **Eschelles** Low necklines **Casaquin**	Combed back from face, smooth and high on top, **toupee** fashion, arranged in a bun on the top or a plait at the back **Tête de mouton** **Bergere,** or **shepherdess hats**				
	1760–1790	**False rumps** **Polonaise** **"Round" gowns** **Redingote dresses** **Chemise à la reine** **Caraçao**	Hairstyles expand to extreme sizes; towering structures expand with feathers, jewels—seemingly anything! By 1780s, height diminishes, but width is retained **Calashes,** or **caleches**				

CHILDREN (PP. 287–289)

Styles for children come into being; after age 11 or 12, adult dress assumed; the practice of swaddling given up by the end of the century in England and America

Muslin from India has impact on children's fashion

Skeleton suit

Boys wear trousers; girls wear simple straight dresses

[A]For 18th-century hairstyles and headdress, *see* Illustrated Table 10.2, p. 286.
[B]For 18th-century accessories, *see* Illustrated Table 10.1, p. 278.

Relationship of Decorative and Fine Arts to Costume

Looking back at the "Decorative and Fine Arts Table" on page 234, choose one figure and describe how it relates to costume from this chapter.

Using the textbook and the "At a Glance" feature of Chapter Ten of this study guide, can you sketch or describe the dress of the following people from the 18th century?

1. Upper-class man of the first half of the 18th century

2. Upper-class man of the second half of the 18th century

3. Man dressed in a banyan

4. Working-class woman wearing a short gown

5. Woman in a *robe `a la Francaise*

6. Woman in a *chemise de la reine*–style dress

FINAL REVIEW QUESTIONS

1. Who at the French court during the 18th century can be said to have influenced fashions? Describe some of the specific ways that that influence was shown.

2. The following words had different meanings in the 18th century than they do today: *undress, nightgown, coat, frock.* What did each mean at that time, compared to the present-day meaning of the same words?

3. What is *Anglomania*? What impact did it have on fashions during the 18th century?

4. How can men's suit styles of the first half of the 18th century be compared with those of the second half? How did styles change, and how did they remain similar?

5. What item supported the silhouette of 18th-century women's dresses?

6. Describe how the silhouette of women's costume changed from the beginning to the last decade of the 18th century. How did hairstyles also change throughout the century?

7. Thorstein Veblen's theory of the leisure classes reflects the theme of ECONOMICS in the 18th century. List some examples of how fashions of the period demonstrated this theory.

8. As it had during previous centuries, foreign trade continued to influence clothing styles in the 18th century. What were a few of the ways that trade influenced fashion during this period?

NOTES

The Nineteenth Century 1800–1900

Read pages 295–306 and complete the following chart.

	TIME PERIOD	KEY EVENTS BY COUNTRY
CHAPTER 11		
CHAPTER 12		
CHAPTER 13		
CHAPTER 14		

After reading pages 295 to 305, can you answer the following questions?

1. In what ways did the following ethnic groups adapt to fashionable dress, and in what ways did they retain their own traditions? (pp. 296–298)

    a.   Native Americans

    b.   Hawaiians

    c.   African-American slaves

2. Describe some of the most common abuses suffered by workers in 19th-century textile and clothing manufacturing industries. (p. 299)

3. What styles described in the Part Five opener reflect the theme of CROSS-CULTURAL INFLUENCE? (pp. 299–300)

4. What changes in men's clothing in the 19th century have led the authors to discuss women's clothing before discussing men's clothing in all of Chapters 11–19? (p. 302)

CHAPTER ELEVEN

The Directoire Period and the Empire Period 1790–1820

HISTORICAL SNAPSHOT

The Directoire and Empire Periods encompass the years from the French Revolution until about 1820. During this time, fashions took on greater symbolic meanings, owing to dramatic social and political upheaval, and differences with previous styles became pronounced. The Directoire Period (c. 1790–1800) includes major events in the French Revolution and the establishment of the Directory, a government by a five-man executive. The Empire Period coincides generally with the period during which Napoleon Bonaparte was head of state, extending his power over all of Europe and defeating all but Great Britain—which remained at war with France until Napoleon's defeat at Waterloo in 1805.

In the United States, the continuing expansion of the American frontier brought Native American and European populations into frequent contact, and European settlers adopted or adapted some forms of Native American dress, although the major styles continued to parallel those of Europe. The Industrial Revolution stimulated the production of lower-cost fabrics, especially those made of cotton in the Southern American states.

MAJOR CONTENT AND THEMES OF THE DIRECTOIRE PERIOD AND THE EMPIRE PERIOD

As you read Chapter Eleven (pp. 307–325), use the space provided to take notes about the chapter. Focus your attention on those areas that your instructor identifies as important. Return to Chapter 1, pages 3–10, and review the concept of theme as a unifying subject and idea related to dress. Try to identify examples of dress that relate to the themes identified in the summary on page 323. These notes will help you answer questions related to the key concepts and learning objectives, and later prepare for tests and projects.

Based on your reading of Chapter Eleven and your notes about the Directoire Period and the Empire Period, can you answer the following questions?

1. POLITICS and POLITICAL CONFLICT are two themes addressed in the chapter. What are some specific examples of costumes that relate to these themes? (pp. 308–309, 323)

2. Describe the parallels between the arts and the costume styles of the Directoire and Empire Periods. (pp. 313–314)

3. Why in this and subsequent chapters is information about women's costume presented before that of men, whereas in previous chapters men's costume is presented first? (pp. 314, 315)

4. According to the textbook, what are some examples of survivals of Empire-style costume ideas in later periods? (p. 324)

Directoire and Empire Periods

	GARMENTS (PP. 315–316, 319–321)	HAIR AND HEADDRESS[A] (PP. 317, 321)	FOOTWEAR (PP. 317–319, 321)	ACCESSORIES AND JEWELRY[B] (PP. 319, 321)	COSMETICS (P. 322)
WOMEN	Women's clothing becomes more complicated and more subject to change Very fashionable women cease wearing corsets in Directoire Period Corsets cut in a straight line without waistline indentation, push breasts up and out Some women use false bosoms made of wax or cotton Cotton or linen drawers Some women place **petticoats** over chemises **Pantalettes** "Grecian-style" **gowns** **Round gowns** **High stomacher dress** **Habit shirt** Low-cut necklines, both round and square Shawls, stoles, cloaks, and capes worn outdoors The **spencer** **Pelisse**	Directoire styles based on Greek prototypes, with hair combed back and gathered in curls around the head; other styles include a short, curly style, *à la victime* or *à la Titus* Jockey caps Influences from Egypt and ancient Greece and Rome Bonnets, **toques**, and "gypsy hats" Mature women wear **day caps** indoors	Shoes in colors that match dresses or **pelisses**; made of leather, velvet, or satin Return of flat shoes and right- and left-cut soles Slippers with criss-cross lacings Calf-high short boots For bad weather, women wear **pattens**, with small platforms of wood or steel that fasten over the shoes	Gloves made of leather, silk, or net **Reticules**, or **indispensibles** Hand-carried items include muffs, parasols, fans, and decorative handkerchiefs Necklaces, earrings, rings, small watches pinned to the dress, brooches, and bracelets in imitation of the Greek and Roman style	
MEN	Linen or cotton drawers Full-cut shirts with high, standing collars, made from linen or cotton **Cravats** **Stocks** A coat, a waistcoat worn beneath the coat, and either breeches or trousers make up the suit Formal and informal dress differs only in quality and color of fabric Coats have tails where the cut-in ends **Pantaloons** **Cossacks** Full overcoats, single- or double-breasted; some with capes at the shoulder Dressing **gown**, or **banyan**, for home, street, and office wear	Men cut their hair short **Top hats** are the predominant style **Bicorne** **Chapeau bras**	Shoes have low, round heels, rounded toes; tie closing gradually supplants buckles Many boot styles named for military heroes True military boots cover front of knee, are open at back of knee	Gloves are short, made of cotton or leather **Quizzing glasses** Rings, decorative watch fobs, and occasionally decorative brooches	Some fashion-conscious men rouge their cheeks, bleach their hands, and use cologne

[A]For women's hairstyles and headdresses in the Empire Period, *see* Illustrated Table 11.1, p. 318.
[B]For Empire Period accessories, *see* Illustrated Table 11.2, p. 320.

Directoire and Empire Periods (cont'd.)

		GARMENTS (PP. 315–316, 319–321)	HAIR AND HEADDRESS[A] (PP. 317, 321)	FOOTWEAR (PP. 317–319, 321)	ACCESSORIES AND JEWELRY[B] (PP. 319, 321)	COSMETICS (P. 322)
CHILDREN (P. 323)	GIRLS	Dresses cut along same lines as those of adult women, but shorter **Pantalettes** under dresses For out-of-doors, shawls and **pelisses**	Small girls wear simple, natural styles Adolescents adopt adult styles Bonnets	Slippers Boots		
	BOYS	Until age 4 or 5, boys wear dresses with skirts similar to those of girls By age 4 or 5, boys don trousers under skirts; by 6 or 7, they wear a **skeleton suit** After age 11 or 12, boys dress the same as men	Hair worn long or short	Slippers Boots		

[A]For women's hairstyles and headdresses in the Empire Period, *see* Illustrated Table 11.1, p. 318.
[B]For Empire Period accessories, *see* Illustrated Table 11.2, p. 320.

Relationship of Decorative and Fine Arts to Costume

Looking back at the "Decorative and Fine Arts Table" on page 304, choose one figure and describe how it relates to costume from this chapter.

Using the textbook and the "At a Glance" feature of Chapter Eleven of this study guide, can you sketch or describe the dress of the following people from the Directoire Period and the Empire Period?

1. Incroyable

2. Woman dressed in style typical of the Directoire Period, c. 1800

3. Woman of about 1817

4. Man of about 1815

1. Explore some of the ways that the themes of POLITICS and POLITICAL CONFLICT are evident in dress during the French Revolution. For example, how was clothing used to directly express political positions? Did clothing also express political positions indirectly during the war?

2. Compare and contrast men's clothing styles of the Empire Period with those of the 18th century. What major changes in men's dress occurred at this time?

3. Recall from Chapter 1, page 6, the term cultural authentication. What items of dress during the Empire Period can be identified as showing cultural authentication of the clothing of Native Americans? What items of European dress were embraced and transformed by Native Hawaiians?

4. Why was the color white so popular during the Directoire Period?

5. How did women's dress silhouettes change during the Empire Period? What impact did this these changes have on underclothing and accessories?

6. At what stage of children's development did boys' clothing differ from girls' clothing? What were the differences? At what stage of children's development did their clothing differ from that of adults? What were the differences?

NOTES

CHAPTER TWELVE

The Romantic Period 1820–1850

HISTORICAL SNAPSHOT

The term *Romantic* is applied to literature, music, graphic arts, and the dress of about 1820–1840. Romanticism represented a reaction against the formal Classical styles of the 17th and 18th centuries. Romantics were nonconformists who believed in fierce emotion and a mythologized view of the past. The Romantic lifestyle included wearing beards, long hair, and costumes that showed conscious attempts to revive elements of historical dress. The influence of Romanticism declined after the revolution in France (1848–1849).

In England, Parliament extended voting rights to more men, and in 1837, Victoria became queen. In France, the Bourbon monarchy was restored, but unwillingness to make reforms helped lead to the outbreak of revolution in 1848, and a tidal wave of revolution swept over Austria, the German states, and Italy. Meanwhile, in the United States, westward expansion had begun, and by the mid-19th century, the cultivation of cotton dominated the economy of the southern states. Because of cotton, the South was identified with slavery, a condition that separated the South from the North.

During this period, women's magazines included depictions of popular fashions. Some types of ready-made clothes were available for men, but for women, clothing was still largely made by seamstresses or at home.

MAJOR CONTENT AND THEMES OF THE ROMANTIC PERIOD

As you read Chapter Twelve (pp. 327–351), use the space on the left to take notes about the chapter. Focus your attention on those areas that your instructor identifies as important. Return to Chapter 1, pages 3–10, and review the concept of *theme* as a unifying subject and idea related to dress. Try to identify examples of dress that relate to the themes identified in the summary on page 348. These notes will help you answer questions related to the key concepts and learning objectives, and later prepare for tests and projects.

Based on your reading of Chapter Twelve and your notes about the major themes of the Romantic Period, can you answer the following questions?

1. Compare the kinds of clothing required by an affluent woman of the Romantic Period with the kinds of clothing required by a working-class woman. How were those differences related to socioeconomic status? (p. 330)

2. Costume historians have additional sources to consult when studying the dress of this and all subsequent periods. What are these additional historical sources? (pp. 330–331)

3. Describe the clothing of slaves in the United States before the Civil War. According to the textbook, how was the clothing personalized? (pp. 346–348)

4. How does the clothing of this period of the 19th century reflect the theme of GENDER DIFFERENCES? (p. 350)

5. What distinctive element of women's clothing from the Romantic Period was revived in later periods? What type of costume featured this revival? (p. 350)

The Romantic Period: 1820–1850

	GARMENTS (PP. 331–338, 340–343)	HAIR AND HEADDRESS[A] (PP. 334, 336–338, 343–344)	FOOTWEAR (PP. 340, 344)	ACCESSORIES AND JEWELRY[B] (PP. 334, 340, 344)	COSMETICS AND GROOMING (P. 340)
WOMEN	1820–1825 is a period of transition between Empire and Romantic styles Transition involves changes in waistline placement and the development of large sleeves Undergarments include **chemises**, drawers, **stays**, and **petticoats** **Bustles** **Morning dresses, day dresses, promenade** or **walking dresses**, and **carriage dresses** Diverse sleeves have many names **Pelisse-robe** Silhouette of dresses become more subdued beginning in the late 1830s **Gilet corsage** Trimmings include **ruchings**, flounces, scallops, and cordings Pelisse replaced by a variety of shawls and mantles and other outdoor garments in the 1830s	Hair worn parted at the center front After 1824, elaborate loops or plaits of false hair are added **À la Chinoise** style **Day caps, capotes**, and hair ornaments worn by adults In the 1830s and 1840s, fashionable bonnet styles include **drawn bonnets** and **capotes**	Most shoes are of the slipper type Stockings knitted of cotton, silk, or worsted wool **Galoshes** introduced in the late 1840s	Separate garments are used as accessories to dresses **Chemisettes** or **tuckers, pelerines, fichu pelerines, santon**, and **canezou** In the 1820s and 1830s, women wear gold chains with lockets, scent bottles, or crosses attached **Chatelaines** **Mitts** or mittens	Rice powder used to achieve a pale and wan appearance Obvious rouge or other kinds of face paint are not considered "proper"
MEN	Clothing more subdued in color and ornamentation Shirts cut with deep collars Ultrafashionable "dandies" of the 1820s The name **trousers** gradually replaces *pantaloons* **Spencer** replaced by **greatcoats** and **box coats** following the 1820s **Paletot** **Chesterfield** **Mackintosh** Changes in cut and style of men's suits and coat styles in the decade after 1840	Hair worn loosely waved or in loose curls Beards return to fashion around 1825 **Top hat** **Derby hat** or **bowler**	Shoes have square toes and low heels Bedroom slippers worn at home Elastic gaiters invented in the 1840s	Gloves are the most important accessory for men Little jewelry other than cravat pins, brooches, watches, jeweled shirt buttons and studs, and decorative gold watch chains and watches	

[A]For selected Romantic Period hairstyles and headdress, *see* Illustrated Table 12.1, p. 337.

[B]For Romantic Period accessories, *see* Illustrated Table 12.2, p. 339.

The Romantic Period: 1820–1850 (cont'd.)

		GARMENTS (PP. 331–338, 340–343)	HAIR AND HEADDRESS[A] (PP. 334, 336–338, 343–344)	FOOTWEAR (PP. 340, 344)	ACCESSORIES AND JEWELRY[B] (PP. 334, 340, 344)	COSMETICS AND GROOMING (P. 340)
CHILDREN (PP. 344–347)	GIRLS	A return to more constricting styles after greater freedom of the Empire Period Girls' dresses are similar to those of women, but shorter and with low necklines and short sleeves	Hat, bonnet, or starched lingerie cap	Ankle-high boots White cotton stockings		
	BOYS	Until age 5 or 6, most boys are dressed in skirts, after which they are put into trousers **Eton suit** remains a basic style for the rest of the century **Tunic suit**		Ankle-high boots White cotton stockings		
SLAVES IN NORTH AMERICA (PP. 347–348)		Practices vary, but the pattern is often to issue two outfits of clothing per year—one for the warm months and one for the cold months Fabrics coarse and harsh, either homespun or purchased inexpensively For women, a "frock" or "robe" with a simple, sleeveless and collarless bodice joined to a skirt Men wear loose-fitting shirts over loose pantaloons or short breeches Those who work in the house are dressed more fashionably than field hands				

[A]For selected Romantic Period hairstyles and headdress, *see* Illustrated Table 12.1, p. 337.
[B]For Romantic Period accessories, *see* Illustrated Table 12.2, p. 339.

Relationship of Decorative and Fine Arts to Costume

Looking back at the "Decorative and Fine Arts Table" on page 304, choose one figure and describe how it relates to costume from this chapter.

Using the textbook and the "At a Glance" feature of Chapter Twelve of this study guide, can you sketch or describe the dress of the following people from the Romantic Period?

1. Woman of the 1820s wearing daytime dress

2. Woman of about 1835 wearing daytime dress

3. Woman of about 1842 wearing evening dress

4. Man of about 1830 in an overcoat

5. Man of about 1845 dressed for daytime

6. Small girl of about 1839

1. An important theme running through costume history is that of RELATIONSHIPS BETWEEN COSTUME AND DEVELOPMENTS IN THE FINE AND APPLIED ARTS. Describe how the Romantic movement in the arts was reflected in costume of the Romantic Period.

2. What were a few of the differences between the clothing of affluent women and the clothing of women from lower socioeconomic classes? How did these differences relate to differences in their respective social roles?

3. What are the sources of information about costume after the 1830s that provide costume historians with more extensive and more accurate information about styles than in earlier periods? What are the strengths and weaknesses of these resources?

4. Fashion is often described as evolving, rather than changing radically. Describe the gradual evolution in women's dresses between 1820 and 1850, noting changes in hemlines, waistline placement, sleeve shapes, and skirt shapes.

5. How did changes in the silhouette of men's coats parallel changes in the silhouette of women's dresses during the Romantic Period?

6. How did changes in the silhouette of children's clothing parallel changes in the silhouette of women's dresses during the Romantic Period?

7. What are some of the sources that costume historians have used to gather information about clothing worn by enslaved persons? What generalizations about their dress can we make based upon this information?

NOTES

CHAPTER THIRTEEN

The Crinoline Period 1850–1869

HISTORICAL SNAPSHOT

This period was named for the cage crinoline, a device for holding out women's skirts. In England during this era, the accepted ideal of womanhood was wife and mother, epitomized by the country's young queen, Victoria. England enjoyed prosperity and industrial growth, and other nations strove to emulate its success. In France, Charles Frederick Worth, considered to be the first designer of the French *haute couture*, helped Paris become the fashion center of Europe. The city had passed its bloody days of revolution, and during the Second Empire France regained the leadership of Europe and Paris became a world capital. Although France's fortunes started to decline by the 1860s, Paris remained the world's fashion capital.

In the United States, the nation was bound together by a growing network of turnpikes, rivers, canals, and railroads. Manufacturing output in the northeastern states surpassed the value of southern agricultural products. The foundations of public school education had been established, and the women's rights movement had begun. The discovery of gold in California in 1848 sparked a Gold Rush, and the United States was divided by the Civil War (1861–1865).

MAJOR CONTENT AND THEMES OF THE CRINOLINE PERIOD

As you read Chapter Thirteen (pp. 353–377), use the space on the left to take notes about the chapter. Focus your attention on those areas that your instructor identifies as important. Return to Chapter 1, pages 3–10, and review the concept of *theme* as a unifying subject and idea related to dress. Try to identify examples of dress that relate to the themes identified in the summary on page 374. These notes will help you answer questions related to the key concepts and learning objectives, and later prepare for tests and projects.

Based on your reading of Chapter Thirteen and your notes about the major themes of the Crinoline Period, can you answer the following questions?

1. Charles Worth is considered to be an important figure in the history of costume. Who was he and what is his legacy? (p. 354)

2. What were some of the ways that American women in the South coped with clothing shortages during the later years of the Civil War? (p. 357)

3. In your own words, explain why the sewing machine was important during the American Civil War. How did the Civil War help popularize the sewing machine? (p. 358)

4. What role did TECHNOLOGY play in the development of women's underwear, textiles, and the ready-to-wear clothing industry? (pp. 358, 360–361)

5. How did the hoop that supported hoop skirts discourage the adoption of the "Bloomer" costume? According to the textbook, what group of women initially adopted the Bloomer costume? Did the costume survive beyond this period and if so, where? (pp. 358–359)

6. List a few Crinoline Period costume styles for men and women that survived in later periods. (p. 376)

The Crinoline Period: 1850–1869

	GARMENTS[A] (PP. 361-366, 370-374)	HAIR AND HEADDRESS[B] (PP. 366-367, 372-373)	FOOTWEAR (PP. 367, 372-373)	ACCESSORIES AND JEWELRY[C] (PP. 367, 372)	COSMETICS (PP. 367-370)
WOMEN	Basic silhouette fits closely through the bodice to the waist, then the skirt widens into a full round or dome shape **Chemise** and drawers worn under a **corset** and a **hoop**; over the **corset**, a **corset cover** or **camisole** A **petticoat** on top of the **hoop** Red **Garibaldi** blouse popular in the 1860s One- or two-piece dresses **Princess dress** Varying sleeve types Skirts widen in the 1850s and 1860s In the late 1860s, skirts are gored and have higher waistlines and fullness concentrated at the back Popular outdoor garments are the **mantle**, **pardessus**, **paletot**, **burnous**, and **zouave**	Hair parted in the center and drawn over the ears into a bun or plaits at the back of the head During daytime, hair confined in a **snood** Small hats fashionable by the 1860s	Stockings made of cotton or silk Shoes worn for daytime have square toes and low heels Evening shoes made of white kid or satin Boots closed with lacing, buttons, or elastic sides	Popular hand-carried accessories include handkerchiefs, parasols, folding fans, and small muffs **Swiss belts** Fashionable jewelry includes coral, cameos, **cabochon stones**, colored glass, and jet	"Paint" considered in bad taste among "ladies of quality"
MEN	Cotton or linen underdrawers and undervest Suits are made up of coats, waistcoats (vests), and **trousers** Popular coat styles: **sack jacket** and **reefers**, or **pea jackets** **Knickerbockers** (later shortened to **knickers**) appear after 1850	Men wear their hair fairly short, and either curly or waved Long, full side whiskers are considered stylish **Top hats** **Stetson hat** created in 1865	Laced shoes, short boots with elastic sides or buttoned or laced closings; long boots	Canes, umbrellas with decorative handles, gloves Watches and watch chains, tie pins, rings, and a variety of ornamental buttons and studs	

[A]For selected Crinoline Period undergarments, *see* Illustrated Table 13.1, p. 364.

[B]For typical women's hairstyles and headdress in the Crinoline Period, *see* Illustrated Table 13.2, p. 368.

[C]For Crinoline Period accessories, *see* Illustrated Table 13.3, p. 369.

The Crinoline Period: 1850–1869 (cont'd.)

		GARMENTS[A] (PP. 361–366, 370-374)	HAIR AND HEADDRESS[B] (PP. 366–367, 372–373)	FOOTWEAR (PP. 367, 372–373)	ACCESSORIES AND JEWELRY[C] (PP. 367, 372)	COSMETICS (PP. 367–370)
CHILDREN	GIRLS	Infants dressed in long **gowns** Girls wear shorter versions of the styles adopted by adult women; skirts lengthen as girls grow Older girls wear **hoops**	Infants wear caps indoors and out Hair often dressed in tight ringlets around the face	Slippers or ankle-high boots		
	BOYS	Infants dressed in long **gowns** Trousers or short pants similar to men's clothing **Knickerbocker** suits Sailor suits	Infants wear caps indoors and out Short hair Caps, straw sailor hats, small pillboxes, and smaller versions of men's hats	Slippers or ankle-high boots		

[A]For selected Crinoline Period undergarments, *see* Illustrated Table 13.1, p. 364.
[B]For typical women's hairstyles and headdress in the Crinoline Period, *see* Illustrated Table 13.2, p. 368.
[C]For Crinoline Period accessories, *see* Illustrated Table 13.3, p. 369.

Relationship of Decorative and Fine Arts to Costume

Looking back at the "Decorative and Fine Arts Table" on page 304, choose one figure and describe how it relates to costume from this chapter.

Using the textbook and the "At a Glance" feature of Chapter Thirteen of this study guide, can you sketch or describe the dress of the following people from the Crinoline Period?

1. Woman in a Garibaldi blouse of about the 1860s

2. Woman in an evening dress of the 1860s

3. Woman dressed for outdoors during the 1860s

4. Man in a sack jacket in the 1850s

5. Man dressed in a frock coat of about the 1850s

6. Boy in a suit with a zouave jacket

FINAL REVIEW QUESTIONS

1. What were some of the innovations that Charles Worth (and his sons) brought to the fashion design industry in France?

2. Why is the Crinoline Period sometimes called the "Second Empire"?

3. TECHNOLOGY is a theme that is related to dress styles throughout history. What technological advances affected clothing during the Crinoline Period? What was the impact of those advancements?

4. Several items of women's and children's costume were inspired by clothing worn by the military during the Crinoline Period. What were these items, and what were the military events?

5. Compare men's current daytime clothing styles with those of the Crinoline Period, noting the similarities and differences.

6. Men and boys both wore knickers, or knickerbockers. In what situations did men wear them? In what situations did boys wear them?

7. What elements of Crinoline Period styles might be considered as "revivals" of earlier styles?

NOTES

CHAPTER FOURTEEN

The Bustle Period and the Nineties

1870–1900

HISTORICAL SNAPSHOT

The Bustle Period derived its name from the device that provided the shaping for a skirt silhouette with marked back fullness. The last decade of the 19th century was called "The Gay Nineties" or, in France, "La Belle Époque." Both names convey a sense of fun and good humor.

Ruled by Queen Victoria, the British Empire had grown to include lands across the world, and industrial England was in the midst of a great economic boom. There was a gradual extension of voting rights, and passage of legislation to clean up the slums and improve sanitary conditions. Although the social conventions of Victorian England continued, there were signs of changing attitudes. In France the Second Empire was replaced by the Third Republic, and in the United States the Civil War had ended and industrialization, urbanization, and immigration were continuing apace.

During this period, women were beginning to enter the workforce and participate in sports, especially bicycling. The invention of the sewing machine facilitated the movement to mass production, which contributed to the development of the garment industry and ready-made clothes. Many stores had begun to publish mail-order catalogs.

MAJOR CONTENT AND THEMES OF THE BUSTLE PERIOD AND THE NINETIES

As you read Chapter Fourteen (pp. 379–409), use the space provided to take notes about the chapter. Focus your attention on those areas that your instructor identifies as important. Return to Chapter 1, pages 3–10, and review the concept of *theme* as a unifying subject and idea related to dress. Try to identify examples of dress that relate to the themes identified in the summary on page 406–408. These notes will help you answer questions related to the key concepts and learning objectives, and later prepare for tests and projects.

Based on your reading of Chapter Fourteen and your notes about the major themes of the Bustle Period and the Nineties, can you answer the following questions?

1. How did fashion styles of this period reflect increased numbers of women both in the workforce and in active sports? (pp. 380–382)

2. List some factors that contributed to the development of the ready-to-wear industry. In your own words, explain how these factors were related to the theme of TECHNOLOGY. (pp. 382, 406)

3. Describe how the styles of the Aesthetic and Art Nouveau movements were reflected in the costume of this period. (pp. 383–384)

4. Why did advocates of dress reform for women claim dress reform was important? (p. 385)

5. According to the textbook, how many different bustle styles developed between 1870 and 1880? What were the changes in each? (pp. 385–391)

6. Mourning costume customs became rigid in the late Victorian Period. Explain the reason for this, and explain why these customs became less important after World War I. (pp. 405–406)

The Bustle Period and the Nineties: 1870–1900

		GARMENTS[A] (PP. 385–392, 396–400, 401–403)	HAIR AND HEADDRESS[B] (PP. 393, 400, 403)	FOOTWEAR[C] (PP. 393–396, 401, 403)	ACCESSORIES AND JEWELRY[D] (PP. 396, 401, 403)	COSMETICS AND GROOMING (PP. 396, 401)	CLOTHING FOR ACTIVE SPORTS (P. 392)	MOURNING COSTUME (PP. 405–406)
WOMEN	**THE BUSTLE PERIOD: 1870–1890**	The **bustle** provides the shaping for a skirt silhouette, with back fullness; three phases with distinct differences over 20 years **Combination** **Tea gowns** Evening dresses differ from daytime dresses in use of more decorative fabrics, greater ornamentation, and cut of sleeves and necklines **Cuirass bodice** introduced in 1875 Variety of outdoor garments increases	Bangs or curled fringe Hats and bonnets exceedingly elaborate	Embroidered and striped stocking patterns popular Pointed toes and medium-high heels predominate Daytime shoes often match dresses	Evening dress requires gloves that are elbow-length or longer Boas Fans Jewelry used more for evening than for day; brooches sometimes worn with daytime dresses	Face creams, beauty soaps, rice powder, and light scent	Costumes worn for tennis, golf, yachting, or walking are made with bustles and elaborate draperies Dresses for sports are cut slightly shorter **Jersey** Bathing costumes consist of bloomers or trousers with an overskirt and bodice	Widows must wear deep mourning for a year and a day Deepest or first mourning consists of black crape-covered dresses and black accessories
	THE NINETIES	Skirts lose their extreme back fullness, and bodices develop **leg-of-mutton sleeves** Underwear trimmed with lace, tucking, or embroidery New corset shape confines the waist and ends just below the bust **Shirtwaist** styles range from blouses with **leg-of-mutton sleeves** tailored to look like a man's shirt to styles covered with lace, embroidery, and frills **Tailor-mades** are matching jackets and skirts, worn with a blouse Capes with high puffs at the shoulders	"Gibson Girl" favors an arrangement with deep, soft waves around the face **Pompadour** Hats worn only out-of-doors	Shoes generally have slightly rounded toes, medium-high heels	Gloves are worn short during the day, long in the evening Boas remain popular Art Nouveau design influence in jewelry	A little tinting added to face powder and face creams	**Knickers** worn with a fitted jacket proposed as cycling costume Bathing costumes often have large, puffed sleeves of elbow length, narrow waistlines, and full, bell-shaped skirts	Widows must wear deep mourning costumes for a year and a day Deepest or first mourning consists of black crape-covered dresses and black accessories

[A] For selected undergarments, *see* Illustrated Table 14.1, pp. 388–389.

[B] For selected hats and hairstyles for women, *see* Illustrated Table 14.2, p. 394.

[C] For selected footwear, *see* Illustrated Table 14.3, p. 395.

[D] For Bustle Period and Nineties accessories, *see* Illustrated Table 14.4, p. 398.

The Bustle Period and the Nineties: 1870–1900 (cont'd.)

	GARMENTS[A] (PP. 385–392, 396–400, 401–403)	HAIR AND HEADDRESS[B] (PP. 393, 400, 403)	FOOTWEAR[C] (PP. 393–396, 401, 403)	ACCESSORIES AND JEWELRY[D] (PP. 396, 401, 403)	COSMETICS AND GROOMING (PP. 396, 401)	CLOTHING FOR ACTIVE SPORTS (P. 392)	MOURNING COSTUME (PP. 405–406)
MEN	**Union suits** Frock coats remain fashionable until the late 1890s and are then replaced by morning coats **Norfolk jacket** Shirts for formal daytime wear have stiff, starched shirt fronts Tuxedo introduced in the 1880s Major styles of outdoor garments are chesterfield or top frock coats, the **inverness cape**, and the **ulster**	Short hair with a side part Mustaches are popular, worn with side whiskers or a beard **Top hats**; bowlers, or derbies; **fedoras**; and **homburgs** popular hat styles	Lace-up patent leather shoes for day or evening dress Elastic-sided shoes, oxfords, and gymnastic shoes popular	Gloves and walking sticks Jewelry not considered masculine; exceptions are tie pins, watches, shirt studs, and cuff links		Straw boater hats worn for sports	Required to wear only a black armband over the suit sleeve

CHILDREN (PP. 403–405)	
	Infants and young children of both sexes are dressed alike
	Girls' dresses are like those of adult women in silhouette, but are shorter in length
	Styles for girls include Russian blouses, Scotch plaid costumes, smocked dresses, pinafores, and sailor dresses
	In the 1880s, boys' knickers are like short trousers, ending at the knee
	Kate Greenaway styles
	Little Lord Fauntleroy suits
	Once boys are out of skirts, their hair is cut short
	Girls' hair is long; natural waves are encouraged

[A]For selected undergarments, *see* Illustrated Table 14.1, pp. 388–389.

[B]For selected hats and hairstyles for women, *see* Illustrated Table 14.2, p. 394.

[C]For selected footwear, *see* Illustrated Table 14.3, p. 395.

[D]For Bustle Period and Nineties accessories, *see* Illustrated Table 14.4, p. 398.

Relationship of Decorative and Fine Ats to Costume

Looking back at the "Decorative and Fine Arts Table" on page 304, choose one figure and describe how it relates to costume from this chapter.

Using the textbook and the "At a Glance" feature of Chapter Fourteen of this study guide, can you sketch or describe the dress of the following people from the Bustle Period and the Nineties?

1. Man in the new style of evening dress of the 1880s

2. Woman in daytime dress of the 1870s

3. Woman in a dolman mantle of the 1870s

4. Man in a business suit of the 1890s

5. Woman in a tailor-made costume of the 1890s

6. Woman dressed for bicycling in the 1890s

7. Young boy dressed in a Little Lord Fauntleroy suit

1. What impact did the participation of women in sports have on women's clothing styles between 1870 and 1900? To what extent was clothing designed and worn for specific sports?

2. Several factors led to increased manufacturing of ready-to-wear clothing during the last decades of the 19th century. What were a few of these factors?

3. Explain how the Aesthetic Movement sought reform both in the arts and in clothing. List some specific costume items that originated either directly or indirectly from the Aesthetic Movement, and explain their origins.

4. What was Art Nouveau? How did the Art Nouveau influence appear in costume?

5. Trace the evolution of bustle skirt styles from 1870 to 1890, describing the changes in the skirt silhouette. What elements of the Bustle Period can be seen in skirts of the 1890s?

6. Explain how changes in the shape of women's garments from the Crinoline Period to the Bustle Period resulted in changes in the corsets of each period.

7. Compare men's clothing at the end of the 19th century with men's clothing at the beginning of the 19th century. What major changes and innovations do you see during this period? Which changes have persisted up to the present time, and which have not?

8. List the stages that girls and boys went through as they progressed toward wearing adult clothing in the late 19th century.

NOTES

PART SIX

Twentieth–Twenty-first Century 1900–2008

Read pages 411–416 and complete the following chart.

CHAPTER TITLE	TIME PERIOD
CHAPTER 15	
CHAPTER 16	
CHAPTER 17	
CHAPTER 18	
CHAPTER 19	

After reading pages 411 to 416, can you answer the following questions?

1. Why did photography largely replace art in showing current fashions? (pp. 412–413)

2. When did the production of fashion become globalized, and what impact did it have on international fashion? (p. 413)

3. Which additional media sources developed in the 20th century, and what influence did they have on the study of 20th-century fashions? (p. 413)

CHAPTER FIFTEEN

The Edwardian Period and World War I 1900–1920

HISTORICAL SNAPSHOT

Prince Edward's name is generally applied to the first decade of the century. He brought to England an emphasis on social life and fashion. In France, innovative designers such as Paul Poiret and Mariano Fortuny established themselves as fashion leaders in *haute couture*, and a relaxed political system led to a remarkable number of creative artists and scientists active at this time.

During this period, women, now more fully engaged in work outside the home, agitated for the right to vote—efforts that were successful in the United States at the end of the second decade. Technological advances made mass production of clothing possible, and ready-to-wear could be brought in large department stores or by mail order. The automobile industry boomed.

Peace was shattered when World War I erupted in Europe in 1914. The war influenced styles of clothing in Europe and America in a number of ways, the most prominent being a move by women into more practical clothes, and shortages of fabrics and certain dyestuffs for coloring.

MAJOR CONTENT AND THEMES OF THE EDWARDIAN PERIOD AND WORLD WAR I

As you read Chapter Fifteen (pp. 417–445), use the space to take notes about the chapter. Focus your attention on those areas that your instructor identifies as important. Return to Chapter 1, pages 3–10, and review the concept of *theme* as a unifying subject and idea related to dress. Try to identify examples of dress that relate to the themes identified in the summary on page 443. These notes will help you answer questions related to the key concepts and learning objectives, and later prepare for tests and projects.

Based on your reading of Chapter Fifteen and your notes about the major themes of the Edwardian Period and World War I, can you answer the following questions?

1. According to the textbook, who were two of the most influential fashion designers of this period? List some notable characteristics of their designs. (pp. 419, 421–422)

2. How is the theme of CROSS-CULTURAL INFLUENCES reflected in fashion during this period? (p. 422)

3. If you were to research the styles of the period from 1900 to 1920, what sources could you use? (p. 424)

4. How did most men obtain their clothing between 1900 and 1920? How did most women obtain their clothing during this same period? (p. 424)

5. Some types of textiles were restricted in their use because of World War I. List a few of the restricted types, and note why they were restricted. In your own words, describe how this situation influenced dress of that era. (p. 420)

The Edwardian Period and World War I: 1900–1920

	GARMENTS[A] (PP. 421–422, 424–428, 432–435, 437–442)	HAIR AND HEADDRESS[B] (PP. 428, 434–436, 440–441)	FOOTWEAR[C] (PP. 430, 436, 441)	ACCESSORIES AND JEWELRY[D] (PP. 430–432, 441)
WOMEN	Japanese, Chinese, and Far Eastern influences From c. 1900 to 1909, Edwardian styles, with emphasis on an S-shaped silhouette **Lingerie dress** **Brassieres** From 1909 to 1911, a narrow, straight skirt predominates Poiret's **hobble skirts** By 1910–1920, skirts shorten and widen Military influence during wartime **Pullovers** become popular after 1915 Fortuny's **Delphos gowns** Coats, cloaks, and capes as outdoor garments Bloomers for sports	The **pompadour** has hair built high in front and at the sides around the face First permanent wave in 1904 1900–1908: Large-brimmed **picture hats**, lavishly decorated Hair ornaments include feathers, jeweled combs, and small skullcaps of pearls (Juliet caps) After 1908, face veils popular	"Louis"-style shoes have pointed toes; long, slender lines; and heels about two- to two-and-a-half inches high	Important accessories are large, flat muffs and suede or leather daytime handbags or beaded evening bags Fans Ruffles **Art Nouveau** influence
MEN	Undergarments: union suits and drawers Suit: jacket, vest, trousers Tuxedo-style jackets for evening Outdoor wear favors **topcoats**, **chesterfields**, **mackintoshes**, and **trench coats** Sportswear includes **blazers**, **jodhpurs**, and **knickers**	Popular hats for men: **top hats**, **homburgs**, **derbies**, caps, **Stetson hats**, **straw boaters**, and **Panama hats**	Oxfords and laced high shoes for daytime; patent leather slippers for evening	Gloves, handkerchiefs, scarves
CHILDREN	Girls: lingerie dresses, with waistline low on hip, knee length For school, sailor dresses, navy blue serge, **pinafores** 1900–1910: young boys in skirts until age 3 or 4; 1910–1920: rompers and **knickers** Older boys wear sailor suits, **Eton suits**, long pants	Girls wear their hair in long ringlets School-age boys wear short hair		

[A]For selected undergarments for women, men, and children, 1900–1920, *see* Illustrated Table 15.1, p. 426.

[B]For selected hairstyles and hats for women, 1900–1920, *see* Illustrated Table 15.2, p. 429.

[C]For selected footwear for women, 1900–1920, *see* Illustrated Table 15.3, p. 130.

[D]For accessories, 1900–1920, *see* Illustrated Table 15.4, p. 131.

Relationship of Decorative and Fine Arts to Costume

Looking back at the "Decorative and Fine Arts Table" on page 414, choose one figure and describe how it relates to costume from this chapter.

Using the textbook and the "At a Glance" feature of Chapter Fifteen of this study guide, can you sketch or describe the dress of the following people from the Edwardian Period and World War I?

1. Woman of about 1905 dressed for shopping

2. Woman of about 1917 dressed for shopping

3. Woman of about 1910 dressed for bicycling

4. Man of about 1910 dressed for a formal evening occasion

5. Man of about 1913 dressed for a white-collar job

6. Girl about age 8 in 1917

1. The theme of POLITICAL CONFLICT was reflected in dress of the period. What were some specific styles in garments that were influenced by World War I? List also a few specific items of dress that resulted from World War I.

2. Who was Paul Poiret? Describe some of the ways he affected fashion.

3. How did Fortuny's designs differ from those of his contemporaries?

4. What developments in costume can be seen as being related to the increased popularity of the automobile?

5. What media were used during 1900–1920 to spread current information about fashion trends?

6. Women's dress silhouettes continued to evolve from 1900 to 1918. Describe this evolution, noting what influences from earlier costume periods can be seen in these changes.

7. Describe some of the specific changes in children's clothing from 1900 to 1920 that reflected a trend toward greater practicality.

158 | SURVEY OF HISTORIC COSTUME *study guide*

NOTES

NOTES

CHAPTER SIXTEEN

The Twenties, Thirties, and World War II 1920–1947

HISTORICAL SNAPSHOT

The Twenties were characterized by prosperity, changing social mores, and radical changes in clothing for women that paralleled changes in social roles. Flying took on new importance, and passenger air service was beginning by the end of the decade. In America, the chain store took root during this era. Toward the end of the decade the bubble of 1920s prosperity burst, and the Unites States and Europe sank into the period now known as The Great Depression. Although unemployment was widespread, there were still individuals and families who retained their wealth and partook in luxurious lifestyles.

World War II began on September 1, 1939, with the German invasion of Poland. When access to French designers was cut off by the war, American designers were featured in the fashion press. The United States joined the war after the Japanese attack on Pearl Harbor in 1941. To support the war effort, scarce goods were rationed, and guidelines called the "L-85 Regulations" restricted the quantity of cloth that could be used in clothing. Many fabrics available before the war were in short supply. Women who worked in factory jobs formerly held by men required special kinds of clothing.

Beginning with talking pictures in 1927, the popularity of movies skyrocketed, and the film star soon became a major fashion influence.

MAJOR CONTENT AND THEMES OF THE TWENTIES, THIRTIES, AND WORLD WAR II

As you read Chapter Sixteen (pp. 447–493), use the space provided to take notes about the chapter. Focus your attention on those areas that your instructor identifies as important. Return to Chapter 1, pages 3–10, and review the concept of *theme* as a unifying subject and idea related to dress. Try to identify examples of dress that relate to the themes identified in the summary on page 490. These notes will help you answer questions related to the key concepts and learning objectives, and later prepare for tests and projects.

Based on your reading of Chapter Sixteen and your notes about the Twenties, Thirties, and World War II, can you answer the following questions?

1. Women's costume of the 1920s showed many changes from that of previous eras. What, according to the textbook, were these changes? Explain why these changes were seen as evidence of agitation and unrest. (p. 449)

2. What restrictions were placed on clothing during World War II? (pp. 451, 452)

3. How did movies influence fashions? Give two examples of styles that were inspired by films of this period. (pp. 451, 453)

4. How was the progress of TECHNOLOGY evident in the textile fabrics and the components of garments from 1920 to 1947? (pp. 454–455)

5. Name three influential haute couture designers discussed in this chapter. What were their most notable contributions? (pp. 455–457)

6. In your own words, describe the differences between the **haute couture** and the American clothing industry. List two important American designers mentioned in the textbook, as well as the kinds of designs they were known for. (pp. 457, 459–461)

7. What is an example of a recently revived fashion element from the 1920s, 1930s, or 1940–1947? (p. 492)

The Twenties: 1920–1929

	GARMENTS[A] (PP. 462–467, 480–485)	SPORTSWEAR AND CLOTHING FOR ACTIVE SPORTS (PP. 474–478)	HAIR AND HEADDRESS[B] (PP. 467–469)	FOOTWEAR (PP. 469, 486–487)	ACCESSORIES AND JEWELRY[C] (P. 478)	COSMETICS AND GROOMING (PP. 478–480)
WOMEN	Drawers or knickers become **panties** in the 1920s **Cami-knickers, step-ins**, or **teddies** 1920s silhouette: straight, with a dropped waistline Steady rise in skirt hemline until the end of the decade, when lengths drop Chanel suit **Ensembles** of matching dresses and coats or matching skirts, overblouses, and coats Art Deco influence Beading a popular means of ornamentation for evening dresses "Clutch" coats	Raccoon coats for motoring and football games Sweaters, worn long and belted low, popular as sportswear. "Spectator sports styles" Specific costumes for sports, such as tennis, swimming, and skiing	Women wear their hair cropped or **shingled**, and in **bobs** The *cloche* style is the predominant hat form **"Headache bands"** with jewels and feathers Turbans	Tan or flesh-colored silk and rayon stockings Pumps with a strap across the instep or T-shaped straps, oxfords, and Russian-style wide-topped boots **Galoshes** worn open and flapping	Fans made of ostrich feathers Jewelry is plentiful, especially long, dangling earrings	Makeup and cosmetics become an accepted part of women's fashion Plucked eyebrows
MEN	No dramatic change in men's dress takes place from the 1920s through the end of World War II English tailoring Business suit: jackets with pronounced waistlines, single- or double- breasted; wide trousers **Oxford bags**	**Sport**, or **casual, jackets** worn with **knickers** or **plus fours** **Polo shirts** **Lacoste® knit tennis shirt** introduced	Hair pomades Pencil-thin mustaches **Fedoras, derbies, homburgs, straw boaters, Panama hats**, and sports caps continue to be popular hat styles	Oxfords the predominant footwear style	Gloves, handkerchiefs, scarves, umbrellas, and canes Watches, tie pins, shirt studs, cuff links, and rings	
CHILDREN/ TEENAGERS	Young girls' dresses are unfitted Custom of dressing small boys in blue and small girls in pink begins Small boys no longer dress in skirts Boys wear long, belted jackets or **Norfolk jackets** **Sleepers** Specific marketing to teens Bathing suits follow adult styles					

[A]For selected undergarments for women, men, and boys, 1920–1947, *see* Illustrated Table 16.1, pp. 464–465.

[B]For selected hairstyles and hats for women, 1920–1947, *see* Illustrated Table 16.2, p. 468.

[C]For accessories, 1920–1947, *see* Illustrated Table 16.4, p. 479.

The Thirties and World War II: 1930–1947

	GARMENTS (PP. 469–473, 480–490)	SPORTSWEAR AND CLOTHING FOR ACTIVE SPORTS (PP. 474–478, 484–486)	HAIR AND HEADDRESS (PP. 473–474, 486)	FOOTWEAR (PP. 474, 486–487)	ACCESSORIES AND JEWELRY (PP. 478, 487)	COSMETICS AND GROOMING (PP. 478–480)
WOMEN	Undergarments emphasize curves of the figure One-piece dresses, skirts and blouses, and tailored suits remain daytime staples Hemlines fall in the early 1930s, are again rising by mid-decade Early 1930s: cowl necklines, cape collars, and soft finishes, such as bows and jabots; later 1930s: V-necklines and collared dresses Styles "frozen" during wartime Wartime suit styles feature bolero suits and **Eisenhower jackets** Around 1945, **dirndl skirts** popular Military influence on outerwear	Specific costumes for tennis, swimming, and skiing. Bathing suits with halter tops and low-cut backs **Lastex®** used to make bathing suits **Slacks** become a well-established sportswear item in the 1930s	Early 1930s: short hair, softly waved, with short, turned-up curls around the neck **Pageboy** bob Early 1930s: hats small in scale and often tipped **Snoods** Pillboxes in the 1940s	**Bobby-soxers** **Leg makeup** simulates stockings	Handbags range from large leather bags to dainty, beaded evening bags Scarves an important accessory Gloves Jewelry more subdued	
MEN	No dramatic change in men's dress takes place from the 1920s through the end of World War II **Boxer shorts** introduced in the 1930s **English drape suits** Wartime restrictions on suiting styles, materials, and cuts **T-shirts** **Zoot suits**	**Bush jackets** **Dishrag shirts**, **basque shirts**, **cowboy** and **western shirts**, and **Hawaiian shirts** Wind-resistant jackets for skiing	1930s: hair waved and parted Mustaches out of fashion in the 1940s **Fedoras, derbies, homburgs, straw boaters, Panama hats**, and sports caps continue to be popular hat styles	Argyle, chevron, and diamond-patterned socks Moccasins, sandals, cloth shoes for summer, crepe-soled shoes, **chukka boots,** or ankle-high shoes with a **monk's front** closure style Wartime rationing makes leather shoes scarce	Sunglasses introduced Watches, tie pins, shirt studs, cuff links, and rings	
CHILDREN/ TEENAGERS	Waistlines of dresses return to anatomical placement For school, skirts and blouses Princess-line coats popular Boys' jackets cut like those of adult men Jeans worn by both boys and girls as play and everyday clothing Overalls also made of blue denim Bathing suits follow adult styles					

[A]For selected undergarments for women, men, and boys, 1920–1947, *see* Illustrated Table 16.1, pp. 464–465.

[B]For selected hairstyles and hats for women, 1920–1947, *see* Illustrated Table 16.2, p. 468.

[C]For accessories, 1920–1947, *see* Illustrated Table 16.4, p. 479.

Relationship of Decorative and Fine Arts to Costume

Looking back at the "Decorative and Fine Arts Table" on page 414, choose one figure and describe how it relates to costume from this chapter.

Using the textbook and the "At a Glance" feature of Chapter Sixteen of this study guide, can you sketch or describe the dress of the following people from the Twenties, Thirties, and World War II?

1. Women's evening dress of the mid-1920s

2. Women's daytime dress of the mid-1930s

3. Woman's suit of the World War II period

4. Man's polo coat of the 1920s

5. Young man in a zoot suit

6. Man's suit of the World War II period

FINAL REVIEW QUESTIONS

1. Contrast the economic climate of the 1920s with that of the 1930s. Which differences in clothing styles can be attributed to the economic changes?

2. Women's costume underwent radical changes during the 1920s. List some of the most pronounced changes

3. Summarize the major government-imposed clothing restrictions and rationing for women in the United States during World War II.

4. What were some specific items of dress from 1920 to 1930 that showed influences from each of the following: sports, high society, automobiles, motion pictures, and technology?

5. Name three influential designers of the Paris couture, and describe one of the major contributions each made to fashion.

6. Name two influential American designers, and describe one of the major contributions each made to fashion.

7. Reflect on the theme of RELATIONSHIPS BETWEEN COSTUME AND THE FINE ARTS during the 1920s and 1930s, paying particular attention to the Art Deco and Surrealist movements.

NOTES

CHAPTER SEVENTEEN

The New Look: Fashion Confirmity Prevails 1947–1960

HISTORICAL SNAPSHOT

In 1947, after World War II, Parisian fashion turned in dramatic new directions that the fashion press labeled "The New Look." These styles dominated fashion design until the mid-1950s, when some silhouette changes began to appear.

At the end of World War II, the victorious Allied armies effectively partitioned Europe into pro-Western and pro-Soviet spheres of influence. Divided Europe now became the center of the power struggle known as the Cold War. The United States and the Soviet Union began an "arms race" manufacturing and stockpiling nuclear weapons. The United States went to war with North Korea in 1950. At home, unscrupulous politicians like Joseph McCarthy exploited fears of Communist plots and pursued alleged Communists for political gain. Meanwhile, despite prevailing conformity, the Beatnik movement was a precursor of some of the youthful protest movements of the 1960s.

In the United States, during the Eisenhower administration, the issue of civil rights came to the fore, and in 1954, the Supreme Court overturned the doctrine of "separate but equal" in public education. Despite a series of decisions over the next few years striking down segregation laws, by 1960 only limited progress had been made in ending segregation in the United States.

In post-war years, Western Europe underwent major social changes, and its new urban culture came to resemble that of the United States—white collar, middle class, and oriented toward a consumption economy. Automobile ownership was no longer limited to the wealthy, and this period saw the rapid development of air travel and the transition from national to globally interdependent economies.

MAJOR CONTENT AND THEMES OF THE NEW LOOK

As you read Chapter Seventeen (pp. 495–527), use the space provided to take notes about the chapter. Focus your attention on those areas that your instructor identifies as important. Return to Chapter 1, pages 3–10, and review the concept of *theme* as a unifying subject and idea related to dress. Try to identify examples of dress that relate to the themes identified in the summary on page 525. These notes will help you answer questions related to the key concepts and learning objectives, and later prepare for tests and projects.

Based on your reading of Chapter Seventeen and your notes about The New Look, can you answer the following questions?

1. According to the textbook, how did the migration of Americans into the suburbs influence clothing? Based on your own experience, was this a temporary change or a permanent one? (p. 499)

2. Who were the Teddy Boys? Describe the styles associated with them, and give examples of how these styles influenced other groups. (pp. 499–500)

3. What was the New Look? Which designer introduced these styles? What changes did it bring about? (pp. 502–503, 507)

4. What is the *Chambre Syndicale*? What was required of its members? In your own words, explain what is meant by an "original" sold by a couture house. (p. 502)

5. The fashion industry took on a more international character during the postwar period. Identify some of the ways in which both customers and producers of fashionable goods contributed to the internationalization of fashion. (p. 500–501, 505)

6. How did CHANGES IN PATTERNS OF SOCIAL BEHAVIOR influence fashions that were popular during this period? (p. 525)

7. Which New Look styles influenced fashions in later periods? (p. 525)

The New Look: 1947–1960

	GARMENTSᴬ (PP. 507–513, 519–525)	SPORTSWEAR AND CLOTHING FOR ACTIVE SPORTS (PP. 513–514, 522)	HAIR AND HEADDRESS (PP. 514–515, 522–523)	FOOTWEAR (PP. 515, 523)	ACCESSORIES AND JEWELRYᴮ (PP. 515–516, 523)	COSMETICS (P. 516)
WOMEN	**New Look** (1947–c. 1954) followed by the gradual emergence of a softer, easier style (1954–1960) **New Look** style elements: skirts full or pencil-slim, in much longer lengths; nipped, small waistlines; and round shoulders Undergarments made of synthetic fabrics **Girdles**, or **foundation garments** Maternity clothes 1954–1960: Silhouette changes to unfitted look: **chemise, A-line, trapeze**	**Shrugs** **Houseboy pants** and **pedal pushers** **Bikini** introduced in Europe Cotton golfing dresses Bermuda shorts and narrow slacks in the 1950s	Short hair fashionable with the **New Look** Longer hair in vogue mid-1950s Hats range from small in scale to large-brimmed picture hats	**Nylons** 1940s to mid-1950s: rounded toes and very high heels Mid-1950s: toes more pointed, stiletto heels Increase in casual styles: moccasins, loafers, ballet slippers, and **sneakers**	Gloves Handbags tend to be moderate in size, usually with small handles Costume jewelry	Bright red lipstick Mascara on eyelashes and pencil on eyebrows Colored eye shadow after 1956 Nail polish in shades of pink and red
MEN	Styles for men become more diverse in the 1950s **Boxer shorts,** jockey-type shorts, athletic shirts, and **T-shirts** **Bold Look** Double-breasted suit prevails Era of the **gray flannel suit** **Continental suit**	Ivy League Look favored by college students Sports jackets in tartan plaids, corduroy, Indian madras plaid **Chinos** Bermuda shorts Tailored trunks for swimming	**Flat top** 1950s: longer hairstyle, inspired by the Teddy Boys and Elvis Presley 1950s: **fedora** is the staple of men's head wear Straw hats for summer	Synthetic fibers made one-size, stretch stockings possible Oxfords, brogues, and moccasins	Wristwatches, handkerchiefs, and umbrellas Rings, identification bracelets, cuff links, and tie pins	

CHILDREN
Synthetic and synthetic-blend wash-and-wear fabrics
Knitted **T-shirts** and **polo shirts** with collars for boys and girls
For boys, plaid vests and miniature gray flannel suits
Small girls, ages 1 to 4, dress in loose, yoked dresses
Peter Pan collars
Fads include **poodle skirts**
Enormous variety of children's jackets
Girls' hair tends to be short; boys' hair is cropped or worn in a crew cut

ᴬFor selected undergarments for women, men, and boys, 1947–1960, *see* Illustrated Table 17.1, p. 509.
ᴮFor accessories, 1920–1947, *see* Illustrated Table 17.4, p. 517.

Relationship of Decorative and Fine Arts to Costume

Looking back at the "Decorative and Fine Arts Table" on page 414, choose one figure and describe how it relates to costume from this chapter.

Using the textbook and the "At a Glance" feature of Chapter Seventeen of this study guide, can you sketch or describe the dress of the following people?

1. New Look woman's suit as first introduced by Christian Dior

2. New Look evening gown of the late 1940s

3. Double-breasted man's suit of the postwar years

4. Woman's daytime dress of the late 1950s

5. Man's business suit of the 1950s

6. Adolescent's "poodle skirt"

1. What are a few of the major style features of the New Look? How does the New Look compare with styles from the World War II period?

2. Compare zoot suits with those worn by Teddy Boys of the post–World War II period. How does the theme of SOCIAL GROUP MEMBERSHIP relate to the development of both of these styles?

3. What were some of the changes in textile technology that affected clothing styles in the early 1950s? How did those changes affect styles?

4. Describe television's influence on fashion in its early years. What age group was most influenced by fashions seen on television?

5. Describe the major changes in men's suit styles from the immediate post–World War II period until 1960.

6. Postwar changes and developments influenced the price of fashion items. What were some of these influential changes and developments?

7. How is the theme of TECHNOLOGY, as it relates to textile manufacturing, reflected in some specific styles or trends in children's clothing from this period?

NOTES

CHAPTER EIGHTEEN

The Sixties and Seventies: Style Tribes Emerge 1960–1980

HISTORICAL SNAPSHOT

By the mid-1960s, the European Economic Community (EEC) had created a single market for its economic resources. In contrast, the Soviet Union continued to keep tight control over its satellite states in Eastern Europe. Other notable events of this period include Algerian independence from France in 1962, the assassination of President Kennedy in 1963, the start of the American war in Vietnam in 1965, the assassination of Martin Luther King in 1968, the first moon landing in 1969, the National Environmental Policy Act of 1970, the thaw in relations with China and President Nixon's visit to Beijing in 1972, the 1973 Arab–Israeli "Yom Kippur" war, the Watergate scandal and Nixon's resignation in 1974, and the emergence of Japan as an economic power.

Social protests in the United States grew out of movements protesting the Vietnam War, supporting civil rights and women's rights, and expressing concerns about the environment. The concept of "style tribes," groups that followed styles that diverged from mainstream fashion, emerged in this period. Although the notion of using dress to proclaim an ideology or membership in a specific group obviously did not originate in this period, the tendency for young people to identify with a specific group and set themselves apart greatly accelerated. Hippies, mods, and punks were among the earliest of these groups. It was during this period that jeans became a fashion item, and there was greater acceptance of garments for men and women that are similar.

MAJOR CONTENT AND THEMES OF THE SIXTIES AND SEVENTIES

As you read Chapter Eighteen (pp. 529–577), use the space provided to take notes about the chapter. Focus your attention on those areas that your instructor identifies as important. Return to Chapter 1, pages 3–10, and review the concept of *theme* as a unifying subject and idea related to dress. Try to identify examples of dress that relate to the themes identified in the summary on page 574. These notes will help you answer questions related to the key concepts and learning objectives, and later prepare for tests and projects.

Based on your reading of Chapter Eighteen and your notes about the major themes of the Sixties and the Seventies, can you answer the following questions?

1. How did social protest movements of the 1960s and 1970s influence fashions? Select two movements and use specific examples to show how they influenced fashions. (pp. 533–534)

2. What, according to the textbook, is a "style tribe"? List four style tribes of the 1960s and 1970s and describe the fashions associated with these groups. (pp. 535–538)

3. Identify influences on fashion that resulted from the women's movement and the civil rights movement. (pp. 538–539)

4. What themes from Chapter 1 can you identify that relate to the influences discussed on pages 539–543? (pp. 3–10, 574)

5. The textbook describes two theories of how fashion moves through a society: the "bottom up" theory and the "trickle down" theory. Explain the meaning of each of these terms. (pp. 543–544)

6. What is the meaning of the French term *prêt-à-porter*? Why is this an important change in the fashion industry? (pp. 544–546)

7. What was a fashion reporter's experience in the mid-1960s when she tried to enter New York restaurants and clubs wearing a pantsuit? (p. 545)

The Sixties and Seventies

	GARMENTS[A] (PP. 550–556, 562–570)	SPORTSWEAR AND CLOTHING FOR ACTIVE SPORTS (PP. 556, 566, 570)	HAIR AND HEADDRESS[B] (PP. 557, 566, 571)	FOOTWEAR[C] (PP. 557–561, 566, 571)	ACCESSORIES AND JEWELRY (PP. 561, 567, 571–572)	COSMETICS (PP. 561, 568)
WOMEN	Skimmer Miniskirts and micro minis in the mid-1960s Pantyhose Body stockings and body suits as under/outerwear Palazzo pajamas Granny dresses in the 1970s Maxis Midi skirts and "fluid" silhouettes of the mid-1970s Wrap-dresses Pantsuits Mid-to-late 1970s: nightgowns predominate for sleepwear	Leotards Leg warmers Unitard ski suits Monokini Warm-up suits, running and jogging clothing, and sneakers Tennis clothing, in wide array of colors Thong bathing suit debuts in 1975 Hip huggers, hot pants Pants, designer jeans Shetland wool sweaters T-shirts with messages	Bouffant hairstyles in the early 1960s Long, straight hair from the mid-1960s to the early 1970s Vidal Sassoon helps make the geometric cut a popular alternative to long hair Jacqueline Kennedy's pillbox hat adopted by many women Preference for soft, "natural" style in the 1970s Head scarves, berets, and knit caps Hairstyles grow in volume	Colored and textured stockings, pantyhose, or tights worn with short skirts Early 1970s: platform shoes and clogs Latter half of the decade: slender, more graceful shoes, with comfortable heels Boots an important part of daytime dress throughout the period	Pierced ears Multiple gold chains and gold-wire hoop earrings Diamonds by the yard Large tote bags Square, quilted handbags, with chain shoulder straps Leather accessories Digital watch introduced in 1976	False eyelashes "Natural look" of the early 1970s Lipstick brighter and eye makeup more dramatic in the latter half of the decade Major cosmetic companies develop and market complete lines of skin care products
MEN	Upsurge of interest in fashion for men Mod clothing Nehru jackets "Peacock Revolution" provides colorful options for tuxedos Leisure suits popular in the 1970s Late 1970s: three-piece suit with vest returns Leather coats	Olympic- and race-inspired bathing suits Wind-resistant ski clothes White is predominant color for tennis clothing pre-1970; colors introduced in the early 1970s Sport shirts: T-shirts, polo shirts, turtlenecks, velour pullovers and shirts, and sweatshirts Safari jackets	Moderately long hair, beards, mustaches, and sideburns are accepted styles by close of the 1960s Longer hairstyles persist until the late 1970s, when shorter styles return Hats become much less important	High shoes and boots supplement classic styles in the 1960s Platform shoes in the 1970s Work shoes and sandals enter mainstream after being worn by hippie men	Men wear necklaces with turtleneck styles Hippies wear beads and other decorative jewelry	Number of products for men's hair care expands

[A]For selected undergarments for women and men, 1960–1960, *see* Illustrated Table 18.1, p. 551.
[B]For typical hairstyles and hats for women, 1960–1980, *see* Illustrated Table 18.2, p. 558.
[C]For selected footwear for women and men, 1960–1980, *see* Illustrated Table 18.3, p. 559.

The Sixties and Seventies (cont'd.)

CHILDREN (PP. 572–574)	**GIRLS**	"Classic" styles for infants
		Mod- and hippie-derived styles
		A-line, princess-cut **skimmers**
		Blue jeans, bell-bottom pants, and overalls for play
		Go-go boots for adolescent girls
		Quilted and down-filled jackets, hooded sweatshirts, and vinyl slicker raincoats
		Hair worn long and straight or in an **afro**
	BOYS	"Classic" styles for infants
		Nehru-style and mod-influenced suits
		Knitted **T-shirts** and **polo shirts**
		Bell-bottom jeans
		Quilted and down-filled jackets, hooded sweatshirts, and vinyl slicker raincoats
		Longer hair becomes the predominant style

Relationship of Decorative and Fine Arts to Costume

Looking back at the "Decorative and Fine Arts Table" on page 414, choose one figure and describe how it relates to costume from this chapter.

Using the textbook and the "At a Glance" feature of Chapter Eighteen
of this study guide, can you sketch or describe the dress of the following people from the
Sixties and the Seventies?

1. Woman wearing a **miniskirt**

2. Woman wearing a **midi skirt**

3. Woman wearing a **maxi skirt**

4. Man in a suit with a Nehru jacket

5. Man wearing clothing influenced by "the Peacock Revolution"

6. Man wearing a leisure suit

1. What overall trends in men's clothing styles can be attributed to the influence of the mods and the hippies?

2. Describe how jeans came to be a high-fashion item. Do you think jeans can be used to illustrate the bottom-up theory of fashion change? If so, how?

3. What were some of the fashions that emerged at the time of the civil rights movement of the 1960s? What were the motivations that led many African-Americans to adopt these styles? To what extent did these styles become part of mainstream fashion?

4. What impact did the movement for women's rights have on fashion? Identify some of the resulting style changes that have survived.

5. What are some of the ways that current events in politics, space exploration, and the arts were reflected in fashions from 1960 to 1980?

6. Comparing children's clothing to adults' clothing during this period, determine if there were more similarities than differences between the two. Where did most of the trends in children's clothing originate?

NOTES

CHAPTER NINETEEN

The Eighties, the Nineties, and the Twenty-first Century 1980–2008

HISTORICAL SNAPSHOT

The Berlin Wall fell in 1989 and East and West Germany were reunited in 1990. The Soviet government collapsed in 1991 and the Russian Republic was born. The European Community continued to develop and expand its functions, and by 2008 the European Union (EU) had expanded to include twenty-seven countries. In Asia, Japanese economic power and political influence continued to grow, and Japanese competition in automobiles and electronics forced American producers to cut their payrolls and introduce new technologies. In the 1990s, however, the Japanese economy suffered deflation, lowering consumer prices and wages and forcing a transformation in parts of that country's economy. Despite this, Japan continued to be a leader in both luxury fashion and ready-to-wear. In the United States, notable foreign policy events include the invasion of Panama, the Persian Gulf War, and the passage of the North American Free Trade Agreement (NAFTA). After the attack on the World Trade Center on September 11, 2001, United States forces again invaded Iraq, this time with the announced aim of disarming Saddam Hussein because he was thought to have developed weapons of mass destruction. As of 2010, U.S. troops remain in Afghanistan and Iraq.

The AIDS epidemic was felt in the fashion world with the loss of a number of designers and other professionals. Women's professional successes led some to adopt "power suits." The development and use of computers and the Internet has affected numerous facets of business, industry, education, and personal life. Its impact can be seen in the design and manufacture of clothing, merchandising, and distribution. It has made possible the globalization of the fashion industry. Also during this period, the need to decrease carbon dioxide emissions became recognized internationally, and consumer support for environmentally sound products increased. Almost every social, economic, political, and art trend could be seen to have some connections with fashion.

MAJOR CONTENT AND THEMES OF THE EIGHTIES, THE NINETIES, AND THE 21ST CENTURY

As you read Chapter Nineteen (pp. 579–651), use the space provided to take notes about the chapter. Focus your attention on those areas that your instructor identifies as important. Return to Chapter 1, pages 3–10, and review the concept of *theme* as a unifying subject and idea related to dress. Try to identify examples of dress that relate to the themes identified in the summary on page 646. These notes will help you answer questions related to the key concepts and learning objectives, and later prepare for tests and projects.

Based on your reading of Chapter Nineteen and your notes about the major themes of the Eighties, the Nineties, and the 21st century, can you answer the following questions?

1. What changes in the haute couture took place in this time period? (p. 593) Which American designer was invited to show in the Paris haute couture show in 2001? (pp. 600–601)

2. Sociologist Diana Crane believes that haute couture influences on fashion have been replaced by three major categories of styles. What does she call these three categories of styles, and how does she define them? (pp. 592–593)

3. What is the meaning of each of the following terms, and how does each relate to dress and/or fashion in the 21st century?

    a. Cosplay (pp. 581–582)

    b. Organic textiles (pp. 583–585)

    c. Avatar (pp. 586–587)

    d Spandex (pp. 612–615)

4. According to the textbook, what areas have incorporated the use of high-technology fabrics? In what areas are high-technology fabrics likely to play an increasingly important role in the future? (pp. 612–615)

5. What is the difference between deconstructionist fashion design and minimalist fashion design? (pp. 616–617, 628)

6. What examples can you give of media influences on fashions in the 1980s, 1990s, and after 2000? (p. 609)

The Eighties, Nineties, and Twenty-First Century

		GARMENTS (PP. 616–623, 627–639, 643)	SPORTSWEAR AND CLOTHING FOR ACTIVE SPORTS (PP. 623, 639)	HAIR AND HEADDRESS (PP. 624–625, 635, 639–640)	FOOTWEAR (PP. 625, 635, 640, 643)	ACCESSORIES AND JEWELRY (PP. 627, 635, 640, 643)	COSMETICS AND GROOMING (PP. 627, 641)
WOMEN	1980–1995	1980s and early 1990s: shoulder pads, large sleeves Short skirts and **miniskirts** Tightly fitting spandex dresses; use of lace, and sheer fabrics **Deconstructionist** designs Frilly, feminine underwear Bright, floral-printed rayons Tailored suits Wide variety of evening dresses **Le Pouf** Mid-1990s: dresses with interesting details visible at the back Wrap coats and **trench coats** Late 1990s and 2000s: individuals likely to dress in styles acceptable to their peers **Minimalist** design movement Retro styles Outer garments that look like undergarments Bare midriffs Dress styles include strapless, halter, and one bare shoulder; off-the-shoulder and draped necklines; and camisole tops **Boho** **Cargo pants** and **combat shorts** **Trench coats**	Proliferation of exercise suits Spandex-blended stretch fabrics "High-thigh" cut for bathing suits Stretch tights or leggings worn with large **T-shirts**, sweaters, or **miniskirts** Pants are slender in early 1990s, then widen	Diversity of hair styles Headbands and scrunchies Brightly colored hair dyes for punk styles	Sneakers Revival of vintage styles Doc Martens Stiletto heels Flip-flops, **flats**, and **Crocs**™	1990s: diamond solitaire stud earrings 1990s and early 2000s: **pashmina** shawls 2000s: belts with elaborate buckles and decoration "Status bags" Chandelier earrings Bold and showy gold jewelry	Dark lips, with darker outline Mousses, gels, and sprays help maintain tousled hairstyles Tattoos and body piercing

The Eighties, Nineties, and Twenty-First Century (cont'd.)

	GARMENTS (PP. 616–623, 627–639, 643)	SPORTSWEAR AND CLOTHING FOR ACTIVE SPORTS (PP. 623, 639)	HAIR AND HEADDRESS (PP. 624–625, 635, 639–640)	FOOTWEAR (PP. 625, 635, 640, 643)	ACCESSORIES AND JEWELRY (PP. 627, 635, 640, 643)	COSMETICS AND GROOMING (PP. 627, 641)
MEN	Introduction of casual dress office policies; separates become more important Burberry plaids 1980s: emphasis on suits with Italian styling 2000s: suits are slim and dark in color In addition to dress shirts, men wear variety of shirt types with suits Suspenders Linen jackets, black leather **Perfecto motorcycle jackets**	Thermal underwear for cold weather sports Warm-up suits Loose-fitting snowboarding gear Spandex bicycle shorts **T-shirts** and sweatshirts with words or phrases, cartoon characters, sports logos By late 1980s, trouser fronts have pleated fullness and a loose, easy fit; by 1996, pleats are disappearing Casual pants influenced by hip hop style: full, baggy, low on the hip	Shorter hair predominates in the 1980s **Stetson**-style and snap-brim felt hats 1990s: baseball hats and **trucker's caps**	Sneakers, western boots, and hiking and walking shoes 1990s: wing-tipped styles, two-tone shoes, loafers, and sporty oxfords	Wider ties, in the late 1980s and 1990s Gold chains and earrings	Fragrances and after-shave lotions Shaved head and goatee **Soul patch**
CHILDREN (PP. 641–645)	High-priced, high-fashion lines of clothing for children of all ages throughout the period 1980s: vivid, multicolored clothing styles Mid-1990s: newborn infants are wearing caps to reduce heat loss from their heads 1990s: rompers and coveralls for infants Very colorful clothes, in addition to pastels, for very young children School uniforms Logo **T-shirts** Sweatshirt dresses, jumpers, dresses with dropped waistlines, bare midriffs, revival of bell-bottom pants Backpacks **Wheelys** introduced in the 2000s					

Relationship of Decorative and Fine Arts to Costume

Looking back at the "Decorative and Fine Arts Table" on page 414, choose one figure and describe how it relates to costume from this chapter.

Using the textbook and the "At a Glance" feature of Chapter Nineteen of this study guide, can you sketch or describe the dress of the following people from the Eighties, the Nineties, and the 21st century?

1. Woman's daytime dress or suit from the 1980s

2. Woman's outerwear garment designed to look like underwear

3. An example of a retro style for women

4. Man's business suit of about 1990

5. Man in casual dress for business of about 2000

6. Style worn for fitness activities by men and women

1. How did the energy crises of the 1970s and other environmental concerns influence clothing styles and practices in the period from 1960 to 2008?

2. In what ways did changes in women's social and economic roles from 1960 to 2008 affect fashions during this same period?

3. Describe the relationship between the French haute couture and the prêt-à-porter as it existed in the 1990s. What part does each of these play in the origin and distribution of fashionable clothes? Compare this to the roles of each in the period of the New Look styles.

4. When did Japanese fashion design gain international prominence? List a few characteristics of these designs, and describe what impact they had on fashion trends of that time and now.

5. It is often said that social elites set styles. Do you agree or disagree with this statement as it applies to clothing from 1980 to 2008? Support your argument using specific examples.

6. Compare clothing for active sports for men and women around 1900 with clothing for active sports for men and women around 2000. What similarities and what differences do you see in the functions of the clothes for active sports from each of these periods?

7. What general trends in men's clothing are evident from the end of World War II to 2008?

8. Identify styles from 1980 to 2008 that are clearly inspired by styles from an earlier period.

9. Read the "Modern Influences Table" on page 649. Also review examples throughout the book of historical costume and modern dress showing historical influence. Does it seem that designers ever make exact copies of earlier styles? Give reasons and examples to support your answer.

10. Now that you have read and learned about costume history, do you agree or disagree with the idea in the last paragraph of Chapter Nineteen (pp. 649–650), where the authors compare contemporary fashion to a moving river that divides, crosses, comes together again, and separates, but continues to move on? How would you express this idea in your own words?

11. Retro styles play an important part in fashions of this period. Select one example of a retro style that you believe relates to one of the themes discussed in Chapter 1, pages 3–10, and explain that relationship.

GLOSSARY

#s

501 jeans: Jeans manufactured by Levi Strauss Company; the number 501 was the lot number given to jeans in 1890 by the manufacturer

A

A-line: A style of dresses or skirts, introduced in the 1950s and 1960s, that is fitted at the top and flares wider and unfitted toward the bottom, a shape similar to the letter A

à la Chinoise: Women's hairstyle of the Romantic Period, created by pulling back and side hair into a knot at the top of the head, while hair at the forehead and temples was arranged in curls

abolla: A cloak made from a folded rectangle fastening on the right shoulder that distinguished officers from ordinary soldiers in ancient Rome

acetate: Generic category for fibers manufactured from cellulose materials such as wood chips; characterized by a crisp hand and a high luster

Aesthetic Movement: A popularized form of Pre-Raphaelite philosophy (see *Pre-Raphaelite*) that attracted painters, designers, craftsman, poets, and writers

afiche: A round brooch from the early Middle Ages used to close the top of the outer tunic, bliaut, or surcote; also called *fermail*

afro: A hair style first adopted by African-Americans in the 1960s in which hair that has a natural tight curl is allowed to assume its natural shape

aiguillettes: Small, jeweled metal points used as fasteners

alb: A long, white early-Medieval tunic worn by priests; had narrow sleeves and a slit for the head, and was tied with a belt

amice: A strip of linen placed around the shoulders and tied in position to form a collar; worn by priests saying mass in the early Middle Ages

amulet: Charm worn around the neck to ward off evil

anakalypteria: Ritual unveiling of a bride in ancient Greece

Anglomania: In the 18th century, a French fad for English things

anime: Japanese animation

Art Nouveau: In the late 18th and early 19th centuries, a movement in which artists and artisans attempted to develop a style having no roots in earlier artistic forms; characterized by sinuous, curved lines, contorted natural forms, and a sense of movement

artificial silk: Term used before 1925 to describe rayon and acetate; also called *art silk*

ascot: Tie with wide ends that was worn with one end looped over the other and held in place with a tie pin

athletic shirt: Man's sleeveless undershirt with low, round neckline; also worn for gym and sports

avatar: A character representing oneself

B

baby boomers: The 76 million Americans born between 1946 and 1964

Balagny cloak: Circular cape of the 17th century, which hung over one shoulder, often secured with a cord that passed under the wide collar

ballerina length: Evening dresses with hemline placement at mid-calf

balteus: Ancient Roman toga style bringing the section under the right arm higher and twisting the top into a sort of belt-like band, thereby eliminating the *umbo*

bagpipe sleeve: Sleeve style used during the late Middle Ages that widened from the shoulder to form a full, hanging pouch below a tight cuff

band: See *falling band*

band collar: Collar appearing in fashions of the early 2000s that stands up around the neck and may close with buttons at the front or back

banyan: See *Indian gown*

barbette: A woman's headdress used during the early Middle Ages, consisting of a linen cloth that stretched down from the temple, under the chin, and up to the other side of the head, and was worn with a fillet

barege: An attractive silk and wool blended fabric, relatively sheer, crisp, and lightweight; popular in the 19th century

Baroque style: Artistic style from the end of the 16th century to the middle of the 18th century; emphasized lavish ornamentation, free and flowing lines, and flat and curved forms

bases: Separate short skirts worn with a jacket or doublet for civil dress, or over armor for military dress; made from a series of lined and stiffened gores; persisted in civilian dress well into the mid-16th century, and over armor for even longer

basque: The extension of a 17th-century bodice below the waistline

basque shirt: Striped, wide crew-necked shirt popular in the 1930s

battle jacket: Waist-length Army jacket worn in World War II with two breast pockets, fitted waistband, zippered fly-closing, and turn-down collar with revers; also called *Eisenhower jacket*

batwing sleeve: Long sleeve cut with deep armhole extending almost to the waist and tight at the wrist, creating a winglike appearance; a variation of the dolman sleeve

bavolet: A ruffle at the back of the neck of a bonnet to keep the sun off the neck

Bayeux Tapestry: An embroidered wall hanging from the late 11th century that was one of the earliest and most important sources of information about the appearance of medieval armor; depicts the events leading to the Battle of Hastings, which took place in 1066

beatniks: Social group that first appeared in the latter part of the 1950s; characterized by eccentric habits of dress and grooming, including beards, ponytails, and black clothes, especially turtlenecks and berets for men and leotards, tights, and ballet slippers for women

bed hair: Tousled hair

bergere: Large, flat straw hat from the 18th century with low crown and wide brim that sometimes tied under the chin; see also *shepherdess hat*

bertha: Wide, deep collar following the neckline

biggins: Child's cap similar to a coif

bias cut: A technique for cutting clothing to utilize the diagonal direction of the cloth, which has greater stretch

bicorne: Name given by costume historians to an 18th-century hat in the shape of a crescent, with the front and back brims pressed against each other, making points on either side

bikini: Two-piece swimsuit introduced in 1946 by designer Jacques Heim

birrus: A cloak resembling a modern, hooded poncho, cut full and with an opening through which the head was slipped; used in ancient Rome

bishop sleeve: Made with a row of vertical pleats at the shoulder that released into a soft, full sleeve gathered to a fitted cuff at the wrist; popular until 1840; during the Edwardian Period, referred to a sleeve gathered into the *armscye* (armhole) and full below the elbow with fabric puffed or pouched at the wrist

blazer: In the 19th century, referred to a single-breasted sport jacket in a solid color or striped; now made double breasted, in many colors, as well as with varying types of pockets; generally worn with contrasting trousers

bliaut gironé: A close-fitting garment with an upper section joined to a skirt, worn by men and women during the 12th century

blue war crown: Worn by Egyptian pharaohs to symbolize military power or when going to war; made of molded leather and decorated with gold sequins with a *uraeus* at the center front

bob: 1920s slang for short blunt-cut hair, either with bangs or bare forehead

bobbin lace: A complex textile originating in the last half of the 16th century; created by twisting or knotting together linen, silk, or cotton on a series of threads held on bobbins; the resulting lace was held in place with pins set in a pillow; also called *pillow lace*

bobby-soxers: Slang for teenagers of the 1940s who followed current fashion fads such as bobby socks and saddle shoes

bobby pin: Small flexible piece of metal bent in half with prongs held together by the spring of the metal; worn to keep hair in place or to set hair in pin curls; first appeared in the 1920s

body jewelry: Highly decorative accessories that may be held in place with body piercings; includes elaborate metal jewelry and decorative chains that are designed to be worn on the body, face, and head and over stockings or clothing; became popular in the 1990s

body shirts: Shirts for men fitted by shaping side seams to conform to body lines; introduced in the early 1960s

body stockings: Body-length, knitted stretch underwear for women; introduced in the early 1960s

body suits: Body-length, knitted stretch underwear for women that usually ended at the top of the leg; designed to be worn with the upper section visible as a blouse

boho: Derived from the term "bohemian"; style from early 2000s characterized by vibrant colors, softly flowing fabrics, and combinations of variously patterned fabrics, in part a revival of upscale hippie-influenced clothes of the 1960s

Bold Look: Term introduced for men in October 1948; not a radical change in fashion, but rather a continuation of the English drape cut with greater emphasis on a coordination between shirt and accessories and the suit

bombast: Stuffing made of wool, horsehair, short linen fibers called tow, or bran; used to pad trunk hose and doublets

bonnet rouge: A soft woolen peasant's cap of red color that became a symbol of the French Revolution

boot cuffs: Cuffs on suit coats that reached the elbow; popular in the early 18th century

bottom up theory of fashion: The idea that fashion changes result from the adoption by older or more affluent individuals of styles that originated with groups or individuals who are young, less affluent, or from the counter-culture; see also *trickle down theory of fashion*

bowl crop: Hairstyle used during the late Middle Ages that gives the appearance of an inverted bowl around the top of the head

bowler: British term for a hat from the 1840s and 1850s and after with a stiff, round, bowl-shaped crown and a narrow brim; see also *derby*

box coat: See *curricle coat*

boxer shorts: Underwear introduced in the 1930s; style inspired by professional boxers

braces: British term for suspenders

braies: Undergarment consisting of loose-fitting linen breeches, used in the 10th and 11th centuries; fastened at the waist with a belt

brassiere: A basic item of underwear to support adult women's breasts; the bust supporter of the 1890s was modified to make it more suitable for supporting the fashionable silhouette of the early 1900s; the term continues in use although specific details of its structure changed in different periods

breeches: General term referring to any of a variety of garments worn by men to cover the lower part of the body; first appeared in the Middle Ages

breeching: A ritual carried out in Renaissance England when a boy of age five or six was given his first pair of breeches

briefs: Tight-fitting, short knitted underpants worn by men and boys; also woman's or girl's very short underwear, sometimes made of control stretch fabric with garters added

bulla: For a free-born boy from ancient Rome, locket made of gold, silver, bronze, or leather that contained charms against the evil eye; placed around the infant's neck at the time of naming

bum roll: Padded roll placed around the waist in order to give skirts greater width below the waist; popular in the late 16th century

burnous: A large mantle of about three-quarter length with a hood; popular women's garment in the early 19th century; the name and style were derived from a similar garment worn by Arabs who lived in the Middle Eastern deserts

burrus: See *birrus*

bush jacket: Jacket made of khaki-colored cotton with peaked lapels, single-breasted front, belt, and four large bellows pockets, originally worn on hunting expeditions in Africa in the early 20th century

busk: A device made from a long flat piece of wood or whalebone that was sewn into one or more casings in corsets of the early 16th century

bustle: During the Romantic Period, referred to small down-filled or cotton-filled pads worn by women that tied on around the waist at the back that held out skirts in back; by the Bustle Period, referred to any number of supports added for the full backs of skirts: from 1870–1878, a full bustle was created by manipulation of the drapery at the back of the skirt; from 1878–1883, the narrow, cuirass bodice was used, fullness dropped to below the hips, and a semicircular frame supported the trailing skirts; from 1884–1890, large, rigid, shelf-like bustles were used

byrnie: See *hauberk*

Byzantine Empire: Lasted from 339 A.D. to 1453 A.D.; by the 6th century, covered all of Italy, Greece, Turkey, and the Middle East, as well as parts of Spain, North Africa, and Egypt; influenced all of Europe as the greatest cultural center of the period

C

cabochon stones: Stones cut in convex form but without facets, used in jewelry

calash: An 18th-century hood made large enough to cover the hair, made of a series of semi-hoops sewn into the hood at intervals in order not to crush the hair

caleche: See *calash*

calico: Indian printed cotton fabric popularized in England; name first applied to fine-quality, printed cotton fabrics from Calcutta; later came to be generally applied to a wide variety of colorful, printed cotton fabrics of all qualities

California collar: Shirt collar from the 1930s that had shorter, wider points than the Barrymore collar of the 1920s

cambric: A plain-weave, fine, white linen fabric

camisole: See *corset cover*

cami-knickers: A combination of the camisole and panties, worn by women in the 1920s

camicia: The Italian word for a man's shirt and for a woman's chemise; plural *camicie*

canezou: A small, sleeveless spencer jacket worn over a bodice; or a garment synonymous with the pelerine; by the Crinoline Period, became a term applied to a variety of accessories including fichus, muslin jackets worn over bodices, and chemisette neck fillers (see Chapter Thirteen)

canions: Extensions from the end of the trunk hose to the knees or slightly below, made in either the same color as to trunk hose or a color contrasting with trunk hose; fastened to separate stockings at the bottom; used by men in the late 16th century

canons: Full, wide ruffles attached at the bottom of breeches during the mid-17th century

capote: A bonnet with a soft fabric crown and a stiff brim worn by women in the early 19th century

capri pants: Tight-fitting, three-quarter-length pant worn by women; first appeared in the late 20th century

caraçao: A thigh-length, fitted women's jacket with no waistline that flared below the waist, popular in the late 18th century

cargo pants: Pants with large patch pockets, the curved part of the which extends to the waist and forms a loop though which the belt is pulled; popular in the late 20th and early 21st centuries

carmagnole: A short, dark-colored woolen or cloth jacket that was hip length with fullness at the back, cut rather like a smock; popular during the Directoire Period as part of the "sans culottes" style of the French Revolution

carriage dress: A woman's dress from the Romantic Period suitable for riding in a carriage; conformed with current styles and was frequently trimmed with fur

carriage parasol: A parasol from the Romantic and Crinoline Periods with a folding handle

carrying frocks: Long gowns worn in the 17th century by infants who were not yet able to walk

casaque: An early 17th century men's coat with wide, full sleeves that were wide throughout the body and ended at the thigh or below

casaquin: Thigh-length, fitted women's jacket with no waistline seams that flared below the waist; popular in the early to mid-18th century

cashmere (or kashmir) shawl: Shawl made from the soft hair of the cashmere goat, and woven in Kashmir, a northern province on the Indian subcontinent; incorporated a decorative motif thought to derive from the *boteh*, a stylized representation of the growing shoot of the date palm; first appearance of this shawl in Europe is not certain, but some scholars relate it to the arrival in London in 1765 of a young English woman who had been in Bombay; see also *paisley shawl*

cassock: English term for *casaque*

casual Friday: Working days identified by business or industry when employees can wear casual dress to work; for many companies, the selected day is Friday; first began in late 20th century

casual jacket: Men's jacket cut along the lines of a business suit jacket and worn with contrasting fabric trousers; first appeared in the 1920s; also referred to as a sports jacket

catogan: See *club wig*

chainse: A distinctive type of outer garment for upper-class women of the 12th century made of washable material, probably linen; long and seems to have been pleated

Chambre Syndicale de la Couture Parisienne: An organization of couturiers that is still active in the French haute couture

chameleon fabrics: Fabrics that react to external environmental stimuli by changing color reversibly

chapeau bras: Men's flat, three-cornered hat, evenly cocked or crescent-shaped, made expressly to be carried under the arm; popular during the early 19th century

chasuble: Evolved from the Roman *paenula*; was given up by the laity, but continued to be worn by early Medieval clergy with sides cut shorter to allow movement of the arms

chatelaine: Ornamental chains worn by women at the waist from which were suspended useful items such as scissors, thimbles, button hooks, and penknives; popular during the 19th century

chausses: Leg protectors made of mail (armor made of interlocked metal rings); worn by men in the early Middle Ages

chemise: A loose-fitting linen women's undergarment worn very close to the skin; was much like a man's undershirt, except that it was cut longer; first appeared in the early Middle Ages

chemise à la reine: An 18th-century white muslin gown that resembled the chemise undergarment of the period, but, unlike the chemise, had a waistline and a soft, fully gathered skirt

chemisettes: Fillers that raised the necklines of daytime dresses; also known as tuckers

chesterfield: A single- or double-breasted men's coat with no waistline seam, a short vent in the back, no side pleats, and often a velvet collar; popular in the mid-19th century and after

chignon: Bun of hair at the back of the neck

chinos: Washable man's sport pants made of chino cloth, a durable, close-woven, khaki-colored cotton fabric; first appeared in the 1950s

chintz: During the 17th century, referred to hand-painted or printed fabric imported from India that was sometimes glazed; today, generally refers to any printed or dyed cotton-blend fabric with a shiny, glazed surface

chiton: Tunic worn by men and women in ancient Greece that consisted of a rectangle of fabric wrapped around the body and fastened at the shoulders with one or more pins

chlamydon: More complicated form of the woman's diplax used in ancient Greece in which fabric was pleated into a fabric band; see also *diplax*

chlamys: Rectangular cloak of leather or wool pinned over the right or left shoulder; worn by men in ancient Greece over a chiton, especially for traveling, when it could also be used as a blanket

chlanis: Hand-woven tunic presented to a groom by the bride in ancient Greece, symbolizing her mastery of weaving

chopines: Very high platform-soled shoes worn by women throughout Italy and in northern Europe during the Renaissance; worn especially high in Venice

chukka boots: Men's and boy's ankle-high boot laced through two sets of eyelets, made of splits of unlined suede cowhide with a thick crepe-rubber sole; originally worn by polo players and adopted for general wear in the 1950s

circlets: Headbands of gold worn by wealthy women in the early Middle Ages

clavus: Broad purple band that extended vertically from hem to hem across the shoulders on the tunic of a Roman Senator beginning in Republican times; later, referred to any band decorating a tunic; plural *clavi*

clocks: A small design that decorated the sides of white silk stockings in the 1870s

clogs: Shoe style popular during the Middle Ages, the Baroque and Rococo Periods, and the Sixties and Seventies, generally made with a raised sole that often served to keep the foot off the ground

closed mantles: Garments for men in the early Middle Ages consisting of a length of fabric with a slit through which the head could be slipped

clothes: Collective term for all items of apparel worn on the body by men, women, and children

club wig: A style of men's wig from the 18th century in which queues (a lock or pigtail at the back), were doubled up on themselves and tied at the middle to form a loop of hair

coat of plates: Solid military armor from the 14th and 15th centuries; the trunk of the body consisted of a cloth or leather garment lined with metal plates

codpiece: A pouch of fabric sewn into the crotch of hose to accommodate the genitals and tied shut with laces, which made the hose fit properly and enabled men to relieve themselves; first appeared during the Middle Ages; by 1500, had grown to enormous proportions, and became an obvious feature of men's clothing; went out of use by the 17th century

coif: During the 12th century, referred to a men's cap that tied under the chin and was similar to a modern baby's bonnet in shape; gradually disappeared except in the dress of clergy and professions such as medicine; during the early 16th century, referred to a women's cap of white linen or more decorative fabric, with extensions below the ears that covered the side of the face

combat shorts: Thigh-length shorts with two very large patch pockets in front; worn by men and women; first appeared in the late 20th century

combination: A women's undergarment combining the chemise and drawers into one piece; popular during the mid-19th century

commode: See *fontange*

conch: Sheer, gauzelike veil worn by women in the late 16th century, cut the full length of the body from shoulder to floor and worn cape-like over the shoulders

conque: See *conch*

conspicuous consumption: Demonstrating affluence through the acquisition of items that display the wealth of the wearer; term coined by economist and sociologist Thorstein Veblen in his 1899 book, *The Theory of the Leisure Class*

conspicuous leisure: Demonstrating affluence through wearing of encumbering garments, in which it would be difficult to do any menial work; term coined by economist and sociologist Thorstein Veblen in his 1899 book, *The Theory of the Leisure Class*

conspicuous outrage: Economic status could be demonstrated by purchases so outrageous that they showed the buyer had money to spend on something nonfunctional or contrary to expectations for "new" and high-priced garments; term coined by Quentin Bell in his 1973 book, *On Human Finery*

continental suit: Men's suit from the late 1950s with shorter jackets, a closer fit through the torso, and rounded, cutaway jacket front

cony: Small burrowing rodent; trimmings and linings from conys were reserved for the lower classes during the late Middle Ages

cope: A voluminous cape from the early Middle Ages worn by the clergy for processions

copotain: High-crowned, narrow-brimmed, slightly conical hat worn by men and women in the early 17th century; sometimes spelled *capotain*

cornette: A fitted men's hood from the early Middle Ages made with a long, hanging tube of fabric at the back; see also *liripipe*

corn-row braids: A traditional African way of arranging the hair in myriad small braids, worn by women in the 1970s and later worn by both men and women

corselet: A sleeveless, probably decorative form of armor used by men in ancient Egypt during the Middle and New Kingdoms; was either strapless or suspended by small straps from the shoulders

corset: During the late Middle Ages, referred to a round cape used by men that buttoned on the right shoulder and left the right arm free or closed at the center with a chain or ribbon (see Chapter Six); by the 17th century, the term referred to cloth shaped as a bodice that was stiffened, usually with bone, and laced together at front, back, or both; could be used as an under- or outer-garment; see also *busk* and *stay*

corset cover: During the Crinoline Period, a waist-length garment that buttoned down the front, shaped to the figure, with short sleeves; also known as a camisole

cosplay: Term from Japan to used to describe the practice of dressing up as the characters from Japanese *manga* and *anime*; combination of the words *costume* and *play*

cossacks: Peg top trousers made with double straps under the instep worn by men during the early 19th century

costume: Term used by scholars who study historic dress; also used in the theater or in dance or for masquerade

cote: Costume historians use this French term instead of "under tunic" for under tunics worn by both men and women in the 13th century and after; placed over chemise or shirt; see also *surcote*

cote-hardie: Variant of the surcote or outer tunic used by men and women during the 14th century; for men in France, referred to a sleeved garment for outdoor wear; for men in England, referred to a garment for use over the pourpoint, with a distinguishing sleeve that ended at the elbow in front, while hanging down in back as a short tongue or longer flap; for women this garment may have been a fitted gown with a hanging sleeve

cowboy shirt: Shirt worn in the American West during the 19th century; featured a convertible collar, pockets in front, and a V-shaped yoke in front and back, often made of contrasting fabrics; sometimes worn with a neckerchief or a string tie, often closed with grippers; also called *western shirt*

cowl: Originally a monk's hood that either was attached to the tunic or was a separate garment in the early Middle Ages; later became part of lay costume (see Chapter Five)

crackowe: An elongated, exaggeratedly pointed-toed shoe used during the late Middle Ages; also called *poulaine*

cravats: Large scarf-like pieces of fabric separate from the shirt worn instead of collars by men; first appeared in the late 17th century

Crocs®: The waterproof, no-slip shoe, perforated in the front and with a sling back; first appeared in the early 2000s

cross-gaitering: See *leg bandages*

Crusades: In the 11th century, under the urging of Pope Urban II, the European powers launched the first of many wars called Crusades intended to free the holy places of Christendom from the Muslims

cuirass: Close-fitting, shaped armor used in ancient Greece that covered the body and protected the common soldier

cuirass bodice: Extremely tight, boned women's daytime bodice of the mid-1870s extending down over the hips to mold the body

culots: A type of trunk hose worn by men during the late 16th century; not much more than a pad around the hips with very tight-fitting hose

cultural authentication: The process whereby elements of dress of one culture are incorporated into the dress of another

cummerbund: A wide, pleated fabric waistband

curricle coat: Large, loose men's overcoat (or greatcoat) with one or more capes at the shoulder, popular in the 1840s; also known as a box coat

cut-offs: Jeans cut off at the knee and worn as shorts; popular with men and women; first appeared in the 1980s

cyclas: Term used by some costume historians in referring to the surcote; sources vary in defining precisely how, when, and by whom the cyclas was worn

D

DA: Men's longer hairstyle, with sideburns and a duck-tailed shape cut at the back, popular in the 1950s

dagging: Form of decoration used during the late Middle Ages in which edges of the garment were cut into pointed or squared scallops

dalmatic: An ancient Roman tunic used from the 2nd to the 5th centuries that was fuller than earlier tunics, featuring long, wide sleeves

dandy: Term used for a man excessively fond of and overly concerned with clothes

dashiki: A traditional African garment, collarless, wide shirt with kimono-type sleeves; first appeared in the United States during the Civil Rights Movement of the 1960s

day cap: Small muslin or lace caps of the early 19th century worn indoors

day dress: Worn in the last half of the 19th century; suitable for walking and shopping; also called *promenade dress* or *walking dress*

deconstructionists: Designers of the 1990s who took elements of garment construction and put them together in unusual ways, such as seams placed on the outside and fabric edges left unhemmed and raw

deerstalker cap: Checked or tweed men's cap with visors on both the front and back and ear flaps that can be buttoned or tied to the top of the crown; popular in the 1870s

Delphos gown: Pleated gown in which the front and back are laced together, rather than being stitched down the side, reminiscent of ancient Greek dresses; how the pleats were achieved is unknown; patented by designer Mariano Fortuny in 1909

demi-gigot sleeve: Full from shoulder to elbow, then fitted from elbow to wrist, often with an extension over the wrist; popular in the early 19th century

denim: Sturdy, serviceable fabric woven in the twill weave, traditionally made with indigo-blue or brown lengthwise yarns and white crosswise yarns; used in sportswear, work clothes, pants, and jackets and occasionally in high fashion items

derby: American term for a hat with a stiff, round, bowl-shaped crown and a narrow brim; see also *bowler*

designer jeans: Almost twice as expensive as regular jeans, designer jeans prominently display the name of the designer on the posterior of the wearer; first appeared in the late 1970s

diadem: A crown placed on the head that often held flowers, metals, or polished stones

diamonds by the yard: From the 1970s, designer Elsa Peretti's string of gold chain with interspersed diamonds

dimity: A cotton fabric with a woven, lengthwise cord or figure; first appeared in Europe by the end of the 13th century

diplax: Small rectangle of fabric worn by women in ancient Greece, especially over the Ionic chiton, draped in much the same way as the himation

dirndl skirt: A full women's skirt gathered into a waistline to produce a more bouffant effect, sometimes attached to a tight-fitted bodice; popular in the 1940s; it derives from a full-skirted Tyrolean peasant costume originating and still worn in the Austrian and Bavarian Alps

dishrag shirt: Net shirt that first became popular on the French Riviera in the 1930s

ditto suit: Men's suit from the 18th century in which the same fabric is used for pants, jacket, vest, and sometimes cap

dolman: During the 1880s, referred to a semi-fitted women's garment of hip to floor length that was shaped like a coat but had a wide-bottomed sleeve that was part of the body of the garment; was revived in the 1930s and 1940s as a popular women's sleeve construction

double mantles: Either open or closed mantles worn outdoors by women in the early Middle Ages, usually lined in contrasting colors

doublet: Originally a man's close-fitting, sleeveless garment with a padded front; worn during the late Middle Ages, and varying in construction appears even more extensively as part of the Italian Renaissance and in the Baroque Period men's dress; see also *pourpoint* and *gipon*

draped dress: The arrangement of fabric that is loosely folded, pleated, pinned, and/or belted in different ways around the body

draw loom: A special loom from China on which elaborately figured silk fabrics were produced; was in use in Italy by the late Middle Ages, and by 1600 was being used wherever complicated patterns in silk fabrics were being woven

drawers: A 16th-century English term for undergarment that evolved from the braies or breeches

drawn bonnet: A bonnet from the early 19th century made from concentric circles of metal, whalebone, or cane and covered in silk

dreadlocks: Long hair arranged in many long hanging twists; first appeared in the United States in the 1970s

drip dry: Easy-to-care-for fabrics that did not require ironing

drum farthingale: See *French farthingale*

duckbills: Wide men's shoes from the 16th century with decorations including slashing with puffs of fabric pulled through the openings; shape resembled the bill of a duck

duster: Linen men's and women's motoring coats that first appeared in the early 20th century

E

Eisenhower jacket: See *battle jacket*

empire waistline: Ancient Greek–inspired style, revived during the Empire Period, in which the dress is belted high under the bustline

engageants: French term for two or three tiers of lace, or sheer fabric ruffles, used as cuffs on sleeves; during the 18th century and in the Crinoline Period, referred to removable lace or muslin undersleeves (see Chapter Thirteen)

English drape suit: Predominant cut for suits in the 1930s; this style fell softly with a slight drape or wrinkle through the chest and shoulders

English guard's coat: From the 1930s, a dark blue men's coat with wide lapels, an inverted pleat in the back, and a half belt

ensembles: Matching dresses and coats, or matching skirts, overblouses, and coats

eschelles: Ribbons that covered stomachers from the 18th century

Eton crop: A women's hairstyle in the 1920s that was exceptionally closely cropped and dressed like that of a man

Eton suit: A boy's suit from the Romantic Period and after, which derived from the uniform of the Eton School in England; included a short, single-breasted jacket ending at the waist with a cut-square front, wide lapels, and a turned-down collar; also included a necktie, a vest or waistcoat, and trousers

Etruscan: Pre-Roman people who migrated into Italy; by about 800 B.C. they had developed a culture that was superior in skills and artistic production, and more complex in organization, than the culture of the neighboring tribes

eye of Horus: In ancient Egypt, a stylized representation of the human eye that symbolized the moon

F

fade: A men's hairstyle created by African-American, inner-city youth in which the hair is cut very short on the sides, left long on top; it also began to have names, words, or designs shaved on the scalp; first appeared in the 1980s

fake fur: High-pile synthetic fabrics that were first promoted in the 1970s as an environmentally sound alternative to real fur

falcon or **vulture headdress:** Worn by Egyptian queens or goddesses; shaped like a bird of prey with the wings falling down at the side of the head and framing the face

fall: The front opening of men's breeches or trousers from the 18th century where a square, central flap buttoned to the waistline

falling band: A large, flat, turned-down collar attached to a men's shirt during the early 17th century; later made as a separate collar

false rump: During the late 18th century, a pad tied at the back of the waist that supported the fullness of a woman's skirt; filled with cork or other light cushioning materials

fashion: A socio-cultural phenomenon in which a large number of people share a preference for a particular style; the preference lasts for a relatively short time, and then is replaced by another style; generally considered to have begun in Western Europe in the Middle Ages

fashion system: A complex industry, well-developed by the early 20th century, that mass-produced clothing by linking together textile production, clothing design and manufacture, and retail distribution of clothing; has made fashionable clothing available in a wide variety of price ranges

fashionistas: Term coined in the early 2000s for affluent followers of certain fashion designers

feather cut: Short, lightly curled woman's bob, cut in layers, popular in the 1950s and 1960s

fedoras: Low, soft men's hats with the crown creased front to back; first appeared in the 1920s and 1930s

fermail: A round brooch from the early Middle Ages used to close the top of the outer tunic, bliaut, or surcote; also called *afiche*

ferroniere: Chain or band of metal or pearls worn across the forehead, with a jeweled decoration located over the center of the forehead; popular during the late 15th century for women

feudal society: System developed out of the need for protection; to maintain his knights, a lord granted each of them land, called a fief or fiefdom, in exchange for military services; along with the fief came serfs, who worked the land for the lords and knights

fez: Modern-day, traditional Arab head-covering shaped like a truncated cone; worn in southwest Asia or northern Africa

fibula: Pin used in ancient Rome for holding a garment together

fichu: A sheer fabric or lace triangular kerchief worn with a very low neckline during the 18th and 19th centuries

fichu pelerine: A variant of the pelerine used during the Romantic period that had two wide panels or lappets extending down the front of the dress and passed under the belt

fillet: A type of headband; appeared in Mesopotamia, and continued in use throughout the ancient world; revived in the 12th century as standing linen band, rather like a crown, over which a veil might be draped; continued in use well into the 14th century

filling: Yarns that run crosswise in woven fabric; also called *weft*

fish tails: Additional stitched-on free-hanging panel or ruffle in front or back, simulating the tail of a fish

fitchets: Slits in more voluminous outdoor garments of the early Middle Ages; one could put the hands inside for warmth, or reach a purse hung from the belt around the waist of the garment beneath

flammeum: Ancient Roman bridal veil of bright orange that covered the upper part of the bride's face

flannel: A soft wool textile with fibers brushed up to create a napped surface

flat crown: Appears on depictions of Queen Nefertiti, a New Kingdom queen of Egypt, who apparently wore this head covering over a shaved head

flat top: General category of hairstyles in the 1950s, usually for men, in which the tip of the hair is cut to a flat surface

flats: Shoes without heels

folk costume: Dress of the European peasants; had its major development in the 18th and 19th centuries; characterized by the use of traditional textiles and dress forms in order to associate oneself with a specific region or town; stressed conformity and stability rather than change; folk dress in Western Europe diverges from the mainstream of fashionable dress

fontange: An elaborate, tall structure for holding women's hair high on top of the head; made of three or four lace tiers in front, with a cascade of ruffles and bows in the back; popular in the late 18th century; called a *commode* in England and the Americas

foretop: See *toupee*

foundation garment: See *girdle*

four-in-hand: Way of tying today's standard necktie

French bonnet: Men's and women's hat style from the 16th century with a pillbox-like shape and a turned-up brim; some versions had decorative cutout sections in the brim

French farthingale: Women's undergarment used for shaping floor-length dresses; steel or cane spokes of the same diameter were fastened from a topmost hoop at the waistband down; also known as a *wheel farthingale* or *drum farthingale*

frescos: Mural paintings on plaster to decorate the walls and ceilings of buildings; first appeared in the ancient world, with the earliest known example dating back to 1500 B.C., and was utilized throughout Europe and the Middle East ever since

fret: Mesh snood or skullcap used during the late Middle Ages, made of gold mesh or fabric worked in an openwork lattice design and sometimes decorated with jewels

frock: A general term used in many periods for a woman's dress

frock coat: Men's coat from the 18th century cut looser and shorter than a dress coat with a flat, turned-down collar; suitable for country wear and later accepted for formal wear as well

frock overcoat: Cut along the same lines as the frock coat, but longer

fulling: Process whereby wool fabrics are washed and shrunk to produce a dense, close weave

full-bottomed wig: Extremely large man's wig from the 18th century with center part and small sausage curls

G

gabled: Type of coif;linen headcover shape for women during the Northern Renaissance; an English style shaped like a pointed arch

gaiters: See *leg bandages* and *spats*

galligaskins: Wide hose or breeches worn in the 16th and 17th centuries

galosh: In the Baroque and Rococo periods, a flat-soled overshoe with a toe cap for keeping it in place; rubber galoshes for wearing over shoes were introduced in the late 1840s

gambeson: A knight's padded undercoat from the 14th century

gardecorps: An outdoor men's garment from the early Middle Ages with a full, unbelted outer tunic, a hood, and long, full, hanging sleeves, frequently worn with the arms passed through slits above the elbows

Garibaldi blouse: Red, high-necked merino wool shirt worn by women, girls, and boys in the 1860s, with full sleeves gathered into wristbands and a small collar; named after the popular Italian General Giuseppe Garibaldi, who wore a similar red shirt as part of his uniform in the military campaign to unite Italy

garnache: A long men's cloak with capelike sleeves from the early Middle Ages; often lined or collared with fur, this garment was open at the sides under the arms

geometric cut: Haircut by Vidal Sassoon from the 1960s with bold lines and geometric shapes

gibus hat: Collapsible men's top hat popular in the Romantic Period; used in the evening; constructed with a spring so that the hat could be folded flat and carried under the arm

gigot sleeve: Sleeve full at the shoulder, gradually decreasing in size to the wrist where it ended in a fitted cuff; popular in the 1830s; also called *leg-of-mutton sleeve*

gilet corsage: A women's front-buttoning jacket from the Romantic Period, made in imitation of a men's waistcoat

gipon: See *pourpoint* and *doublet*

girdle: In the early Middle Ages, a jeweled belt (see Chapter Five); by the 20th century the term referred to an undergarment worn by women and girls designed to mold the lower torso, and sometimes the legs; may include nonstretchable fabric panels and be made with or without garters; also called *foundation garment*

globalization: A process by which regional economies, societies, and cultures have become integrated through a globe-spanning network of communication and trade

go-go boots: Calf-length white boots worn by girls in the 1960s

going frocks: Shorter dresses worn in the 17th century by children old enough to walk

goring: A process in which the shape of a skirt is created by using a number of panels shaped so that when joined they fit the body in some areas, usually over the hips, and flare out in others, usually toward the bottom

gown: Defined in slightly different ways in different periods, but generally meaning a skirted garment fully covering the upper and lower body and reaching to the ankle or the floor; worn by men or women; after the Renaissance tends to be a used for a woman's garment especially for formal occasions, except when worn by men and women in professions such as the law, religion, or higher education

granny dresses: Long daytime dresses derived from mod and hippie styles and worn in the 1970s

gray flannel suit: A flannel suit for career-minded businessmen popularized in the 1950s

greatcoat: A general term for overcoats; coats could be single- or double-breasted, were often as long as to the ankle, and their collars had a deep roll; coats were made with and without lapels

greaves: In ancient Greece and ancient Rome, referred to leather or metal protectors for the lower legs; in later periods, referred to armor that protected the lower legs

guardaroba: Italian Renaissance set of clothing made up of three garments: two layers of indoor clothing and a mantle for outdoors

guardinfante: A Spanish variation of the French farthingale; wealthy Spanish women took up the style only around the mid-1600s, even though the farthingale was obsolete in the rest of Europe after the second decade of the 17th century; wider from side to side with a long, wide extension of the bodice below the waistline that extended over the top of the skirt; the bodice shoulder line was horizontal and sleeves were full and slashed, ending in fitted cuffs

guild: General term for a league or federation formed by craftsmen in order to regulate the number of artisans and to set quality standards and rates of pay and to regulate working conditions; first appeared in the 11th century

gynaeceum: Workshop in ancient Rome in which women (mainly slaves) carried out weaving, dyeing, and finishing textiles

gypsy hat: In the Directoire and Empire Periods, a woman's hat with a low crown and a moderately wide brim, worn with ribbon tied over the outside of the brim and under the chin

H

habit shirt: A shirt worn by women during the Directoire Period as a fill-in under low necklines

handkerchief skirt: Skirt from the 1920s with hemline cut to fall in points as if made of handkerchiefs

hair à la Titus: A short curly hairstyle popular during the French Revolution; name referenced the short hair depicted on statues of ancient Roman men, such as the Emperor Titus

hair à la victime: A short curly hairstyle popular during the French Revolution; name referenced the short haircuts given to persons about to be guillotined

haubergeon: A short coat of mail worn by a knight over the gambeson during the late Middle Ages

hauberk: Knee-length shirts of mail from the early Middle Ages that were split in front for riding; also called *byrnie*

haute couture: The creation of exclusive, custom-fitted clothing that was designed and made in the atelier of the designer

Hawaiian shirt: Men's sport shirt printed with colorful Hawaiian floral or other local designs; made with a convertible collar and worn outside of trouser; first became popular in the late 1930s

head rail: Scarf; prohibited in Puritan America by religious and secular leaders

headache band: Headband from the 1920s; ones that were jeweled or had tall feathers attached were popular for evening

headband: Strip of leather, cord, or fabric bound around the head horizontally across the forehead; band worn over top of the head from ear to ear as an ornament or to keep hair in place since ancient times

hedgehog hairstyle: A women's hairstyle from the late 18th century that resembled the fur of a hedgehog; the hair was curled full and wide around the face and long locks hung at the back

hemhemet crown: Headdress worn by Egyptian pharaohs, who used it only rarely, on ceremonial occasions, possibly because it was so awkward and unwieldy

Henley shirt: A ribbed-knit undershirt with a buttoned vent at the front of the neck; first appeared during the 1930s; also called *Wallace Beery shirt*

henna: Orange-colored dye from the plant by the same name; ancient Egyptians used it to dye their fingernails

hennin: A tall, exaggerated, steeple-shaped headdress style adopted by Burgundian women at the close of the 14th century

Hercules knot: Belt tied with a double knot worn by a bride in ancient Greece; its loosening took place on her wedding night

herigaut: A full men's garment from the 13th century with long, wide sleeves and a slit below the shoulder in front through which the arm could be slipped, leaving the long, full sleeve hanging behind; also worn by women

heroin chic: Term applied to fashion advertising and magazine photography style of the late 1980s and 1990s in which models appear emaciated, pale, and unkempt, with large circles under their eyes, an appearance likened to that of drug addicts

hidden rivets jeans: Blue jeans with rivets hidden inside the pockets; made by Levi Strauss Company between 1937 and about 1960

high stomacher dress: A dress from the early 19th century with a complex construction in which the bodice was sewn to the skirt at the back only, with side front seams left open to several inches below the waists, and a band or string was located at the front of the waist of the skirt; the bodice often had a pair of under flaps that pinned across the chest, supporting the bust; the outer bodice closed in front by being wrapped across the bosom like a shawl, laced up the front over a short undershirt, or buttoned down the front

high-tech fabrics: Fabrics first produced in the 1980s and 1990s from manufactured fibers with special performance characteristics (e.g., water repellence, strength, stretch, heat resistance)

high-tech footwear: Expensive sneakers for walking in the 1980s that became a status symbol

hijab: A headscarf worn by many Muslim women who follow Islamic teachings; today it is used in combination with acceptably modest contemporary styles

himation: A large rectangle of fabric that wrapped around the body, used by men in ancient Greece; similar to the wrapped shawls of Mesopotamia

hip huggers: Low-slung pants of any style starting below the normal waistline, usually with the belt resting on the hips; first popular in the mid-1960s

hobble skirt: Women's skirt from about 1912 that was rounded over the hips and tapered to the ankle so narrowly that walking was impeded

holoku: A loose-fitting, full-length dress with a high neck and long sleeves that fell from a yoke; became traditional part of Hawaiian dress after missionaries in the early 19th century adapted their own dress style for the overweight Queen Dowager Kalakua

homburg: Man's hat of rather stiff felt with a narrow rolled brim and a lengthwise crease in the crown; popular in the late 19th century and subsequently from time to time

hoodies: Fitted, waist-length cardigan sweaters with attached hoods; first appeared in the late 20th century

hookless fasteners: Zipper device from the early 20th century used in corsets, gloves, sleeping bags, money belts, and tobacco pouches

hoops: Structure of metal, cane, wire, or wooden hoops for holding out women's skirts; the shape of the hoop varied depending on the silhouette that was popular at the time the hoops were worn; see also *panniers*

hose: Stockings; had different lengths and uses in different time periods

hot pants: Slang term describing women's short shorts from the early 1970s; made of luxury fabrics and leather, worn with colored tights and fancy tops both as evening wear and on city streets

houce: A wide-skirted overcoat with winged cape sleeves and two, flat, tongue-shaped lapels at the neck; used during the late Middle Ages; French variation of the garnache

houppelande: Originating as a man's house coat worn over the pourpoint during the late Middle Ages, became a garment for general wear; later also used by women; was fitted over the shoulder, then widened below into deep, tubular folds or pleats, which were held in place by a belt

houppelande à mi-jamb: A mid-calf version of the houppelande for men that appeared in the 1400s

houseboy pants: Pants worn by women in the 1950s that ended at the calf

housse: See *houce*

huke: Garment worn by upper-class men during the late Middle Ages that was shaped much like a tabard, being closed over the shoulders and open at the sides; short versions had a slit at the front for ease when riding; longer versions for walking had no slit

Hussar front or **beak:** A point at the front of a lengthened waistcoat; popular in the 1840s

I

idiot or imbecile sleeve: Extremely full from shoulder to wrist, where it gathered into a fitted cuff; popular in the 1820s and 1830s; name derived from the fact that its construction was similar to that of sleeves used on garments for confining mad persons—a sort of "strait jacket" of the period

Incroyables: The men who affected the most extreme of the Directoire styles, and wore waistcoats that fit loose at the shoulders, excessively tight breeches, and cravats or neckties and collars that covered much of their chins

Indian gown: Comfortable, loose-fitting, often very decorative dressing gown from the 18th century worn by men for indoor and outdoor use

indispensables: See *reticules*

innocente: See *saque*

instita: Term used by Roman writers to describe the distinctive dress of a Roman matron; scholars have disagreed about its construction; some interpret it as a ruffle at the bottom of the tunic that covered the feet; others see it as a dress suspended from sewed-on straps

inverness cape: A large, loose men's overcoat with full sleeves and a cape ending at wrist length, popular during the Crinoline Period

J

jabot: Frilly ruffles of cambric or lace placed at the front of the neck of women's bodices; popular during the Edwardian Period

jack boots: High, rigid men's boots made of heavy leather; popular during the later 17th century

jacket: Term originally used interchangeably with *cote-hardie* during the late Middle Ages; similar in function (though not in cut) to the modern suit jacket, although it was worn with hose rather than with trousers

jeanette: A cross or heart of pearls suspended by a narrow tress of women's hair or a piece of velvet ribbon around the neck; popular during the 1830s

jerkin: In England after 1500, term used synonymously with *jacket*

jersey: A wool knit fabric used for clothing for active sports

Jockey shorts®: Trademark for knitted briefs

jodhpurs: Tight-fitting trousers that reach to the ankle, where they end in a snug cuff; originally imported from the city of Jodhpur, India during the British occupation in the latter half of the 19th century; became popular for military uniforms; after 1940, predominantly used for horseback-riding

Juliet cap: Small skullcap made of rich fabric (or sometimes entirely of pearls, jewels, or metal chain) worn during the Edwardian Period for evening or with wedding veils

jumps: The term applied to loose, unboned bodices worn by women at home during the 18th century to provide relief from tight corseting

justacorps: See *surtouts*

K

kaffiyeh: A black-and-white headscarf associated with the late Yassir Arafat and his Palestinian countrymen; some American men and women adopted this in urban areas during the early 2000s, unaware of its political implications

kalasiris or **calasiris:** Ancient Egyptian fringed tunic, sometimes inaccurately described as a long, tight-fitting sheath-type dress

Kate Greenaway styles: Children's dress based on illustrations by Kate Greenaway, an Aesthetic Movement illustrator of children's books; typical costumes were made of lightweight fabric printed with flowers and styled with a high waistline, puffed sleeves, and ankle-length skirts trimmed with narrow ruffles, worn with ribbon sashes, visible pantalettes, and mob caps or poke bonnets

kaunakes: Skirts worn by both men and women from 3500 to 2500 B.C.; made of fleece or fleece-like materials

kente cloth: Complex, elaborate, multicolored, woven designs made on narrow strip-looms by Ashanti men in Bonwire, Ghana; the cloth is expensive and highly prized; first became popular with African-Americans during the Civil Rights Movement of the 1960s

kiddie couture: The production of expensive clothing for children by well-known designers; first appeared during the late 20th century

kilt: Short skirt worn by Scotsmen; term often used as a means of distinguishing between male and female skirts

knickerbockers: Men's sportswear garment that first appeared after 1850; full and loose, gathered into a band that buckled just below the knee; also worn by preadolescent boys; popular until the 1940s; the term shortened to "knickers"; occasionally worn today, mostly for cross-country skiing

knickers: *See* knickerbockers

knock-off: An item of apparel copied from a more expensive item and generally manufactured from lower-priced components so it can sell at a lower price

kohl: A black paint used by ancient Egyptian women; made of galena, a sulfide of lead

L

L-85 regulations: Guidelines in the United States during World War II that restricted the quantity of cloth that could be used in clothing; savings in fabric were made by eliminating trouser cuffs, extra pockets, and vests with double-breasted suits, and by regulating the width of skirt hems and the length of men's trousers and suit jackets

lace: Differs from either cutwork or filet in that it is constructed entirely from threads, dispensing with any backing fabric; two types include bobbin or pillow lace and needlepoint lace

lacerna: A rectangular cloak from 3rd-century Rome with rounded corners and a hood

lacis: Decorative technique in which the artisan embroiders patterns on a net background

Lacoste® shirt: Introduced in the 1920s, an internationally recognized trademark used extensively on apparel as well as other goods; originally identified the knit shirts manufactured by La Chemise Lacoste of Paris, marked with a small alligator symbol on the left front

laena: A cloak from 3rd-century Rome that was made of a circular cloth folded to a semicircle, thrown over the shoulders, and pinned at the front

lappet: Long, decorative lace or fabric streamer on a garment or headdress

Lastex®: In fashion, refers to a fabric made in the from yarns with a rubber core covered by another fiber; results in a form-fitting and wrinkle-free fabric; often used in bathing suits in the 1930s

latchets: Shoe laces used in the 18th century that crossed the tongue from either side

le pouf: A wide, puffy skirt with a light airy appearance; made in both short and longer styles around 1985, created by Christian Lacroix, designing for Patou

leading strings: Small strings used during the 17th century to help hold a child upright as he or she learned to walk and retained for another two years or so to help control the child's movements

leg bandages: Strips of linen or wool wrapped closely around men's leg to the knee and worn either over the hose or alone; from the early Middle Ages; also called *gaiters*

leg makeup: Because of shortages of fabrics for stockings during World War II, women painted their legs to simulate the color of stockings, including a dark line down the back of the legs in imitation of the seams

leg-of-mutton sleeve: See *gigot sleeve*

leg warmers: Knitted covering for legs extending from the ankle to the knee or above; first appeared in the 1980s

leisure suit: Men's suit styled in knit or woven fabric in a casual style with the jacket similar to a shirt, having a convertible collar, more sporty buttons, and sleeves with single or no cuffs; popular in the 1970s

leotard: A two-piece, knitted, body-hugging garment; originally worn by dancers and acrobats in the 19th century; became part of fashionable dress in the 1960s

lettice: Trimmings and linings used during the late Middle Ages made of ermine and a fur resembling ermine; reserved for women of the nobility

Levis: Sturdy close-fitting workpants that were manufactured by Levi Strauss during the Gold Rush and sold to miners; originally made of heavy-duty canvas, and later from denim dyed blue with indigo

licensing: The sale of the right to use an image or design by the owner (licensor) to a manufacturer (licensee), in return for payment of royalties to the licensor who continues to own the rights to the original image or design

line-for-line copies: American interpretations of Parisian and Italian couture dresses made expressly for American stores; a popular practice in the 1950s

linen: Fiber that is removed from the stems of the flax plant

lingerie dress: White, frilly cotton or linen dress with decorations including tucking, pleating, lace insertions, bands of applied fabric, lace, and embroidery; worn during the Edwardian Period

liripipe: A fitted hood from the early Middle Ages made with a long, hanging tube of fabric at the back; see also *cornette*

Little Lord Fauntleroy suit: A child's suit that consisted of a velvet tunic ending slightly below the waist, tight velvet knickerbockers, a wide sash, and a wide, white lace collar

livery: Costume of nobles and servants of the late Middle Ages, as well as officials of the court and ladies-in-waiting to queens or duchesses; distributed by kings, dukes, and feudal lords; eventually came to mean special uniforms for servants

lock of Horus: Distinctive hairstyle worn by children of Egyptian pharaohs; one lock of hair remained on the left side of the head; also called *lock of youth*

lock of youth: See *lock of Horus*

loincloth: Length of cloth wrapped to cover the genitals

longuette: Radically longer lengths on coats, skirts, and dresses, reaching from below the knee to ankle-length; were an abrupt change from the miniskirts of the late 1960s

lorum: Long, narrow, heavily jeweled scarf that became part of the official insignia of the Byzantine emperor; possibly evolved from the Roman toga with the folded bands

lounge coat: During the Edwardian Period, a loose, comfortable man's jacket that had no waistline, a straight front, center vent in the back, sleeves without cuffs, and a small collar with short lapels

love lock: Long lock of curled hair that was brought forward from the nape of the neck and hung over the chest; worn by men during the mid-17th century

lumber jacket: Waist-length jacket with a bloused effect and rib-knitted bands at waist and cuffs; made of woven plaid wool fabric; originally worn by woodsmen in the lumbering trade; introduced for sportswear in the later 1920s and worn by both adults and children

M

macaroni: Name for young men in 18th-century England who were noted for their brightly colored silks, lace-trimmed coats in the latest silhouette, and fashionable wigs and hats; derived from the Macaroni Club, which was formed those by who affected an interest in continental culture

mackinaw: A hip-length sport jacket made of heavy wool woven in patterns similar to those used for blankets; popular for boys in the Edwardian Period

mackintosh: A waterproof coat made of rubber and cut like a short, loose overcoat; developed in the Romantic Period and continued in use later; became a British synonym for a rain coat

Magyar sleeve: A sleeve cut very full under the arm, tapering to a close fit at the wrist; first appeared in the early Middle Ages

mail: Armor made of interlocking metal rings; first used in the early Middle Ages

mancheron: Very short oversleeve, similar to a large epaulette, worn by women during the Romantic Period

manga: Japanese word for "cartoon"; led young Japanese to engage in *cosplay*, or dressing up as the characters from manga; the practice spread beyond Japan, and over time, the word *cosplay* came to mean dressing as any character

manteau: See *mantua*

mantilla: A large, oblong, fine lace veil first used by Spanish women in the 17th century to cover the hair; is a smaller version of the mantle worn by women during the Medieval Period

mantle: A loose, sleeveless cloak or cape; appeared throughout history

mantlet: A hybrid between a shawl and a short cape with points hanging down at either side of the front; used by women during the Romantic Period; also known as a *shawl mantlet*

mantua: Women's gown of the late 17th and early 18th centuries that was cut in one length from shoulder to hem and worn over a corset and an underskirt; also called *manteau*

mappa: A white linen table napkin used in ancient Rome; guests brought their own napkins when invited to dinner

marcel wave: Artificial wave put in woman's hair with heated curling irons, devised by hairdresser Marcel of France in 1907 and popularized in the 1920s

marie sleeve: Full to the wrist, but tied in at intervals with ribbons or bands; popular for women during the Romantic Period

maxi: Term used for ankle-length daytime skirts, popular with women in the late 1960s as a reaction against miniskirts

Merveilleuses: Women who affected the most extreme of the Directoire Period styles, with long flowing trains, the sheerest of fabrics, necklines cut in some extreme cases to the waistline, and huge, exaggerated jockey-like caps

mixtures: Styles that incorporate components from several cultures

Marco Polo: 11th-century Italian merchant, one of the first Europeans to visit large parts of the Far East, who wrote an influential book about his travels

Medici collar: Open ruffs, almost a cross between a collar and a ruff, stood high behind the head and fastened in front into a wide, square neckline; named for the 16th-century Medici queens of France, Catherine and Marie, during whose reigns this style was popular; style revived in the 18th and 19th centuries

mercerizing: The process of treating cotton fabric with sodium hydroxide, which improves strength, receptivity to dyes, and luster

mi-parti: Men's and women's garments of the late Middle Ages, decorated by sewing together sections of different-colored fabrics; also called *parti-colored*

microfibers: Manufactured filament fiber that measures 10 denier per filament or less

minaret tunic: A wide tunic, boned to hold out the skirt in a full circle and worn over the narrowest of hobble skirts; designed by Paul Poiret for women during the Edwardian Period

micro mini: The shortest of the short skirts; first appeared in the 1960s

midi skirt: A mid-calf-length skirt; first appeared in the 1960s

mini-crinolines: Wide-skirted, short dress popular in the 1980s

minimalists: Influential designers of the late 1990s who made styles in neutral or darker tones that used little ornamentation and had good lines

miniskirt: Term first used in the 1960s to describe a short skirt from 4 to 12 inches above the knee; see also *micro mini*

mitts: Gloves, cut to cover the palm and back of the hand but not the fingers; first appeared in the Romantic Period; also known as *mittens*

mob cap: A women's indoor hat from the early 18th century, with high, puffed-out crowns at the back of the cap and wide, flat borders that encircled the face

mods: Groups of young people in Britain in the mid-1960s; espoused the notion that men and women were entitled to wear handsome and dashing clothing, as well as "long hair, granny glasses, and Edwardian finery"; style gained international attention after being adopted by The Beatles

modeste: The French term for the outer skirt of a women's dress, used in the mid-17th century

monastic: A bias-cut, full tent dress by designer Claire McCardell that, when belted, followed the body contours gracefully; popular in the 1940s and 1950s

monk's front boot: Closed shoe with wide buckled strap over the tongue at the instep rather than lacings; popular for women in the 1940s and for men during World War II, when this style was favored by U.S. Army Air Corps officers

mordant: Substance used to fix dyed colors in fabrics so they do not fade

mourning crape: A black, silk fabric with a crinkled or uneven surface texture; worn by widows for a year and a day as part of the "first mourning" costume of the late 19th century; the modern spelling "crepe" means woven fabrics made from tightly twisted yarns and is not the same fabric as "mourning crape"

muckinder: A handkerchief from the 17th century pinned to the front of a baby or toddler's dress; used like a bib or apron is today

mules: Backless slippers, especially popular for women in the 18th century

muslin: Very fine cotton fabric from Bengal that became enormously popular in the late 18th and early 19th centuries, despite exorbitant prices, due to its softness and drapability; in later periods, less delicate, plain-weave cotton or cotton-blend fabrics have also been called "muslin"

mu'umu'u: Loose-fitting, full dress worn by native Hawaiian women that was adapted from European chemises; worn for swimming and sleeping until the 1930s when it was adopted for street wear

N

nappies: See *tailclouts*

needlepoint lace: Originated in Italy; made by embroidering over base threads arranged in a pattern, and connecting these base threads with a series of small intricate stitches

negro cloth: A coarse, white homespun used in the 18th century for clothing for enslaved people in the West Indies and American South

Nehru jacket: Single-breasted jacket, slightly fitted, with a standing color; introduced in the late 1960s, takes its name from Prime Minister Jawaharlal Nehru of India

nemes headdress: Worn by Egyptian rulers from the Old to the New Kingdom; a scarf-like construction that completely covered the head, was fitted across the temple, hanging down to the shoulder behind the ears, and with a long tail at center back that symbolized a lion's tail

nether stocks: From the 16th century, lower section of a type of men's hose that was sewn together with the upper stocks

New Look: Post–World War II Parisian fashion that took dramatic new directions; introduced by Christian Dior's spring 1947 show, which deviated sharply from the styles of the wartime period; characterized by sharply dropped skirt lengths, enormously full skirts or pencil-slim skirts, a round shoulder-line, and a small, nipped-in waistline; many clothes were made from new and popular "easy-care" synthetic textile fabrics such as nylon, polyester, and acrylics; dominated fashion design until the mid-50s

newmarket: A men's coat from the Romantic Period that sloped gradually to the back from well above the waist

Norfolk jacket: A belted, hip-length men's jacket from the Bustle Period with two box pleats from shoulders to hem, front and back; later on in the same period, also worn by women

nylon: Generic fiber category established by the FTC for a manufactured fiber composed of a long chain of chemicals called polyamides

nylons: Long, sheer stockings made of nylon

nymphides: Special sandals worn by brides in ancient Greece

O

open breeches: During the late 16th century, wide, full style of garment worn by men to cover the lower part of the body

open mantles: Garments made from one piece of fabric that fastened on one shoulder, first used in the 10th century

orarium: White linen handkerchief used in ancient Rome that was slightly larger than the sudarium; became a symbol of rank, and in the late Empire, was worn by upper-class women neatly pleated across the left shoulder or forearm

original: Garment designed and made in the couture house, but is not necessarily the only one of its kind

orphrey: Y-shaped band of embroidery that extended from each shoulder to form a vertical line in the back and front of the chasuble; used by the clergy in the early Middle Ages

Oxford bags: Men's long trousers with very wide cuffed legs; popular in the 1920s, based on the style that began at Oxford University in England

P

paenula: A heavy wool cloak from ancient Rome, semicircular in shape, closed at the front, with a hood

pageboy: Straight hair worn shoulder-length or shorter, with ends curled under very smoothly at the back and sides; popular in the late 1930s

pagoda sleeves: Sleeves from the Crinoline Period that were narrow at the shoulder and expanded abruptly to a wide mouth at the end; sometimes shorter in front, longer in back

pair of bodys: Corset from the 16th century cut into two sections and fastened at the front and back with laces or tapes

paisley shawl: A 19th-century shawl manufactured in the Scottish town of Paisley; made in imitation of the popular cashmere (or Kashmir) shawls from India using less-costly wools and silk; imprinted with a stylized version of the Indian motif called a *boteh*; because of motif's association with the shawls from Paisley, the design is now known as "paisley"; see also *cashmere shawl*

pajamas: One- or two-piece item worn by men and women, originally designed in the Edwardian Period for sleeping; in the 1930s, was also used by women for lounging at home or on the beach, and was a way for them to wear trousers, which previously had been worn exclusively by men

palazzo pajamas: Women's long wide pajamas or culottes with voluminous flared legs and gathered waist; worn for lounging or evening dress in the late 1960s and early 1970s

paletot: A woman's outdoor garment from the Romantic Period, about knee-length and having three capes and slits for the arms; also the name for man's knee-length overcoat

palla: A women's shawl used in ancient Rome; draped over the outer tunic similarly to the toga, casually across the shoulder, or over the head like a veil

pallium: evolved form of the ancient Greek himation; in ancient Rome, was a broad rectangle draped around the shoulders, crossed in front, and held in place with a belt; in the Byzantine Empire, was also called a *lorum*, and consisted of a long, narrow, heavily jeweled scarf that became part of the official insignia of the emperor

paltock: From the early 16th century, English term for a man's doublet to which hose were anchored

paludamentum: A large white or purple cloak similar to the Greek chlamys, worn by emperors or generals in ancient Rome (see Chapter Four); cloak worn by men and women of the Byzantine Empire that fastened over the right shoulder with a jeweled brooch (see Chapter Five)

Panama hat: Hand-woven hat made in Ecuador of fine, expensive straw obtained from the leaves of the jipijapa plant; popular for men in the Edwardian Period; named for the port of sale to which they were shipped before being sold in the United States, Europe, and Asia

panes: Garments ornamented with narrow strips of fabric, under which contrasting linings were placed; especially popular during the Renaissance

panniers: Structure of metal, cane, wire, or wood hoops used in the 18th century for extending a woman's dress at both sides at hip level

pantalettes: Long, straight, white drawers trimmed with rows of lace or tucks at the hem that became fashionable for a short time around 1809; young girls, however, wore pantalettes under dresses from the Romantic Period through to the end of the Crinoline Period

pantaloons: Garment cut from waist to ankle in one piece; at various times it was cut to fit either close to the leg or fuller; by the 19th century the terms *pantaloons* and *trousers* were sometimes used interchangeably.

panties: Term first used in the 1920s for garments worn by women and children under clothing, covering the torso below the waist

pantofles: Heel-less slippers or mules for women, popular in the later 17th century

panty brief: Short underpants worn by women and girls in the 1930s, sometimes made of control stretch fabric with garters added; later known as *briefs*, since they grew shorter in order to fit under active sportswear

pantyhose: Hosiery first marketed around 1960 as an alternative to nylon stockings; made with textured, sheer nylon yarn that follows the design of tights, having stockings and panties cut in one piece

paper dresses: Classification of dresses made from various types of disposable paper or nonwoven fabrics; a fad from 1968

pardessus: A term applied in the Romantic Period to any of a number of garments for outdoor wear that had a defined waistline and sleeves and were from one-half to three-quarters in length

parka: Loose-fitting pull-on jacket made with an attached hood that is sometimes trimmed with real or synthetic fur; worn originally by the Eskimos and introduced during the 1930s for winter sportswear; later versions also opened down the front

parti-colored: See *mi-parti*

pashmina: A synonym for *cashmere* used in the 1990s and after to promote fine-quality cashmere apparel

patches: Small fabric shapes glued to the face during the 17th century to cover imperfections or skin blemishes

pattens: Overshoes from the 18th century that protected against wet and muddy surfaces; similar to *clogs*; were made of matching or other fabrics and had sturdy leather soles, built-up arches, and latchets that tied across the instep to hold the shoe in place; less fashionable versions for working people were made with metal soles and leather fasteners; see also *chopines*

pea jacket: Loose, double-breasted jacket with side vents and small collar; also worn as overcoat during the Crinoline Period; also called *reefer*

Peacock Revolution: Radical changes in men's wear during the 1960s from the conventional clothing to a more relaxed, more creative, colorful, and unconventional style, included turtleneck knit shirts, Nehru jackets, flared pants, Edwardian coats, and other items

peascod belly: Pronounced front of the doublet popular by 1570 that resembled the puffed-out chest of a peacock

pecadil: A row of small, square flaps placed just below the waist of the doublet, popular in the second half of the 16th century

pectorals: Decorative necklaces for men and women used in the ancient world, often featuring semiprecious and precious stones such as carnelian, lapis lazuli, feldspar, and turquoise, as well as religious symbols

pedal pushers: Below-the-knee straight-cut women's pants, often cuffed; popular during World War II for bicycling

peg-top skirt: A skirt from the Edwardian Period cut full at the waistline with darts, gathers, or small unpressed pleats, and tapered inwards from the hip, becoming very narrow at the hem

pelerine: Wide, cape-like collar that extended over the shoulders and down across the bosom; popular for women in the Romantic Period

pelerine-mantlet: A mantlet with a deep cape, coming well over the elbows and having long, broad front lappets worn over, not under, a belt; popular for women in the Romantic Period

pelisse: A 19th-century garment similar to a modern coat; generally full-length, followed the typical Empire silhouette

pelisse-mantle: A double-breasted, sleeved, unfitted coat with wide, flat collar and wide, reversed cuffs, worn during the Crinoline Period

pelisse-robe: Daytime dress, adapted from the pelisse coat, that was fastened down the front with ribbon bows or with hidden hooks and eyes; used from about 1817–1840

Perfecto motorcycle jacket: Black leather jacket that became the symbol for rebellious youth of the 1950s

perizoma: A fitted loincloth garment worn by ancient Greeks and Etruscans that covered much the same area as modern athletic briefs

permanent press: Easy-to-care-for fabrics that appeared in the 1960s; chiefly cotton and cotton-blended with polyester and some wool fabrics, given special treatments to render them more readily washable

pet-en-lair: A short, hip-length dress from the 18th century worn with a separate, gathered skirt

petasos: Wide-brimmed felt hat worn in ancient Greece to provide shade in summer or keep rain off the head

petticoat: In the 16th century, an underskirt worn with an over dress that created an overall silhouette rather like an hourglass; in later periods, an underskirt that was sometimes an invisible undergarment and sometimes a visible garment

petticoat breeches: A skirt or a divided skirt that was cut so full that it gave the appearance of a short skirt, worn by men in the 17th century; also called *rhinegraves*

Phrygian bonnet: Brimless cap with a high padded peak that fell forward; worn in ancient Greece

picture hat: Hat with a large brim framing the face, frequently made of straw; popular for women in the Edwardian Period

pillow lace: See *bobbin lace*

pilos: Narrow-brimmed or brimless hat with a pointed crown, worn in ancient Greece by both men and women

pinafore: During the 17th century, apron-like pinafores replaced bibs; the term derived from the practice of pinning this garment to the front or forepart of a child's gown; also worn over the dresses of young girls from the late 19th century into the 20th century

pinner: From the 18th century, circular cotton or linen cloth cap with single or double frills around the edge, placed flat on the head

placard: See *plastron*

plastron: French word for a stiffened panel with a rounded lower edge; part of the surcote, it joined a wide band encircling the hips to which the skirt was attached; worn during the late Middle Ages; in English, called a *placard*

plumpers: Small balls of wax, placed in the cheeks to give the face a fashionably rounded shape; popular practice in the late 17th century

plus fours: A fuller version of knickers from the 1920s

points: In the late Middle Ages, laces or ties that ended in small metal tips, or "points," and were used to close or join various parts of a garment

polo coat: Coat made of tan camel's hair worn by a British polo team playing exhibition matches in the United States; its popularity continued into the 1930s

polo shirt: Knitted shirts with attached collars and short, buttoned neck vents; style originated as costume for polo players, but was adopted generally for informal wear in the 1920s and after

polonaise: Fashionable from about 1770 to 1785, an overdress and petticoat in which the overskirt was puffed and looped by means of tapes and rings sewn into the skirt, with a hoop or bustle supporting the skirt; in subsequent periods, term was used very broadly to refer to any overskirt puffed or draped over an under layer

pomander: Perfume holder mounted on the long cord of a woman's jeweled belt; used during the 16th century

pomander balls: Small balls of perfume used during the 17th century; enclosed in a decorated, perforated box, or pomander, that might be shaped like an apple

pompadour: A hairstyle from the mid-18th century in which the hair is built high in front and at the sides around the face; named after Madame de Pompadour, mistress of King Louis XV

poodle skirt: Full-circle skirt very popular with adolescents of the late 1940s and early 1950s; was often made of felt and decorated with an appliquéd poodle dog; revived as a style for young girls in the late 20th century

poorboy sweater: Tightly fitting, rib-knit sweaters from the 1960s and 1970s that looked as if they had shrunk

pop art: Short for *popular art*, entered the art world during the 1960s, featured glorified representations of ordinary objects such as soda cans and cartoon figures

postmodernism: A genre of art and literature and especially architecture in reaction against principles and practices of established modernism

poulaine: See *crackowe*

pourpoint: Close-fitting, sleeveless garment with a padded front that originated as military dress; worn by men from the 14th to 17th centuries; also called a *doublet* or *gipon*

power suits: Term used in the late 1980s and 1990s for a man's or woman's tailored suit worn for business

Pre-Raphaelite Movement: A group of Victorian Period painters who took their themes from medieval and Renaissance stories; as they made costumes for their models to wear, the women of the group also adopted these dresses for everyday use

preppy: Style from the 1980s that stressed classic tweed blazers, conservatively cut skirts or trousers, tailored blouses or shirts, and high-quality leather loafers, oxfords, or pumps; style referred to affluent students who attended private preparatory schools, continued on to Ivy League colleges, and later became *yuppies*

prêt-à-porter: French term for *ready-to-wear*; in the mid-1960s, after becoming established in the haute couture, young designers (like Yves Saint Laurent, Pierre Cardin, André Courrèges, and Emanuel Ungaro) who had trained under men like Dior and Balenciaga opened their own establishments and expanded in the direction of ready-to-wear clothes

princess dress: A one-piece style from the Crinoline Period that, instead of having waistline seams, was cut with long, gored sections extending from the shoulder to the floor

princess petticoat: A camisole-type top combined with a petticoat to create a single princess-line garment; see *princess dress*

princess polonaise: Princess-style dress with the outer fabric looped up or draped over the hip

promenade dress: See *day dress*

pschent crown: Worn by Egyptian pharaohs to symbolize rule over Lower and Upper Egypt; consisted of a combination of the red and white crowns of Lower and Upper Egypt

pudding: A special padded cap worn in the 17th century by toddlers learning to walk

pullover: Knitted sweater that pulled over the head; became popular for men and women after 1915

punk style: An exaggerated theatrical look originating in the 1970s; included ripped shirts, leather clothing, and extreme hairstyles

"putting out" system: System popularized for textile industry of the late Middle Ages in which a merchant became the middleman for textile workers, selling the workers the fiber, then buying back the finished cloth, followed by selling it to the fuller, then buying it back; the merchant arranged for dyeing, then sold the completed fabric to agents who sold it at medieval trade fairs

Q

queue: A lock or pigtail at the back of the head; especially popular in the mid-18th century as part of men's wigs

quick response: Computer-based systems created in the 1990s that permit rapid ordering, manufacture, and delivery of goods

quizzing glasses: Magnifying glasses mounted on a handle and worn around the neck; popular in the early 19th century

R

raglan cape: A full overcoat with an innovative sleeve construction popular during the Crinoline Period; the sleeve was joined in a diagonal hole seam running from under the arm to the neckline

raglan sleeves: Sleeve style with seams running from below the arm at front and back to the neck rather than being set into the armhole

rationals: Popular name for full pleated serge bloomers or knickerbockers worn by women for bicycling in the 1890s

rayon: Generic fiber name for manufactured cellulosic fibers regenerated from short cotton fibers or wood chips

red crown: Worn by Egyptian pharaohs to symbolize rule over Lower Egypt

redingote: 18th-century full overcoat originating in England that had a large collar and was worn for riding

redingote dress: 18th-century gown that resembled buttoned redingcote greatcoats with wide lapels or revers at the neck

reefer: See *pea jacket*

reticules: Small handbags, often with a drawstring at the top; popular in the Empire Period; also called *indispensables*

retro: Term coined in the late 20th century for fashions from past eras that are updated as current styles

revers: Lapels used during the late Middle Ages that turned back to show the underside on the V of a gown's bodice; also a contemporary fashion term for this type of lapel

rhinegraves: See *petticoat breeches*

ribbons of childhood: Broad ribbon or tube of fabric—as compared with the narrow, ropelike leading strings—attached to the shoulders of children's dresses in the 17th century

rincinium: Widows in ancient Rome wore this garment instead of a palla for a year of mourning; it was probably dark-colored, but its precise form is unclear

robe à l'Anglaise: An 18th-century dress with a close fit in the front and at the back

robe à la Française: An 18th-century dress with a full, pleated cut at the back and a fitted front

robe battante: See *saque*

robe volante: See *saque*

roc: Loose-fitting gown worn during the late Middle Ages that appears infrequently, seemingly most often in Flemish and German paintings; the bodice was cut with a round neckline with a cascade of gathers or pleats at the very center of the front and back

rockers: Style associated with tough young British men in the late 1950s; costume was a mixture of storm trooper and motorcyclist

Rococo style: Supplanted the Baroque style from 1720 to 1770; considered a refinement of the heavier, more vigorous Baroque expression; marked by S- and C-curves, tracery, scrollwork, and fanciful adaptations of Chinese, classical, and even Gothic lines; smaller and more delicate in scale than the Baroque

rollers: See *staybands*

ropa: A garment of Spanish origin from the 16th century; an outer gown or surcote made either sleeveless or with one of the following types of sleeve: a short puffed sleeve, or a long sleeve puffed at the top and fitted for the rest of the arm's length; possibly derived from Middle Eastern styles

rotonde: A shorter version of the talma mantle popular in the Crinoline Period

round gown: Daytime dress from the late 18th century that did not open at the front to show a petticoat

ruchings: Pleated or gathered strips of fabric; used as ornamental trim; especially popular in the 19th century

ruff: Wide, separate collar used during the second half of the 16th century and the first decades of the 17th century; often made of lace and stiffly starched

S

sack jacket: A loose, comfortable man's jacket with no waistline, straight fronts, center vents in back, sleeves without cuffs, and a small collar with short lapels; originated in the Romantic Period and popular during the Crinoline Period and after; forerunner of the modern sports jacket

sacque: An 18th-century gown that was unbelted, loose from shoulder to floor; also called *robe battante*, *robe volante*, and *innocente*

sacred peplos: Magnificently patterned garment carried in procession to the temple to be placed upon the statue of the Greek goddess Athena

safari jacket: Jacket from the late 1960s and 1970s with peaked lapels, single-breasted front, belt, and four large bellow pockets

sagum: A cloak made from a single layer of thick wool, generally red; worn by ordinary soldiers and by citizens in ancient Rome at time of war

sandalis: See *solae*

sans culottes: Literally meaning "without breeches," was a nickname for revolutionaries who wore trousers (associated with the common people) instead of breeches (associated with the aristocrats) during the French Revolution

santon: For women in the Romantic Period, a silk cravat worn over a ruff

scarab: Popular motif in ancient Egypt that represented the sun god and rebirth

schenti: A wrapped skirt; major garment for men throughout all of Egyptian history; its length, width, and fit varied with different time periods and social classes; also called *shent* or *skent*

secret: The bottom layer of a women's skirt from the 17th century

segmentae: Square or round decorative medallions that were placed in different areas of tunics of the early Middle Ages

selvage: Tightly woven band on either edge of fabric parallel to the warp (lengthwise direction) that prevents fabric from unraveling

sericulture: Silk production process, including how the silkworm was bred, raised, and fed; said to have been brought to Western Europe from China by two monks in the 6th century

set-in sleeves: Sewn-in sleeves, a design feature influenced by military garments during the late Middle Ages

shawl: Woven rectangles or squares of fabric, draped in various ways

shawl-mantle: A loose cloak for women from the Romantic Period, reaching almost to the skirt hem

shawl mantlet: See *mantlet*

sheath dress: In ancient Egypt, a close-fitting women's garment that consisted of a tube of fabric beginning above or below the breasts and ending around the lower calf or ankle that appeared to have one or two straps holding it over the shoulders; in modern times, refers to a tight-fitting dress that follows the line of the body

shent: See *schenti*

shepherdess hat: See *bergere*

shingle: An exceptionally short women's haircut of the 1920s in which the back hair was cut and tapered like that of a man

shirtwaist: A woman's blouse styled like a man's shirt with buttons down the front and a tailored collar, and sometimes worn with a black tie; first important in the 1890s

short gown: A garment from the 18th century similar to a loose jacket or overblouse, worn with a skirt by working class and rural women

shorts suit: A woman's suit from the 1980s consisting of shorts and a matching tailored jacket, worn as an alternative to the skirted suit

shot fabric: Iridescent fabric created by weaving one color in the lengthwise yarns and another in the crosswise yarns

shrugs: Bolero-like cardigans from the 1950s

Silent Generation: Post–World War II and Korean-War generation of young people

sinus: Pocket-like pouch formed from the overfold of the Imperial Roman toga

skeleton suit: Worn by boys older than seven or eight during the 18th and early 19th centuries; consisted of long straight trousers, a white shirt with a wide collar that finished in a ruffled edge, and over the shirt, a jacket that either was a shorter, simplified version of those worn by adults or was cut to the waist and double-breasted

skent: See *schenti*

skimmer: A-line dress or shift that hangs away from the body

skirt: A garment beginning at the waist or slightly below and hanging loosely around the body in varied lengths; in the ancient world and much of the Medieval Period, worn by both men and women; in later periods and in modern Western fashion, generally worn by women, with a few exceptions; see also *wrapped skirt*

slacks: Term usually applied to loose-cut casual pants, not part of a suit

slap soles: A flat sole attached to high-heeled shoes only at the front, not at the heel; a feature of some early 17th-century footwear

slashing: A cut in the fabric through which an underlayer of contrasting colored fabric might be pulled; especially popular during the Renaissance Periods

sleeper: Sleepwear for young children in the form of pajamas with feet

sleeve en bouffant: Alternated places of tightness with puffed-out expansions

slip: Undergarment developed in the 1920s, beginning above the bust, worn by women and girls, usually held in place with shoulder straps; length is long or short in relation to the dress worn on top

sloppy joes: Large, loose pullovers worn by adolescents in the mid-1940s

slops: Style of trunk hose that sloped gradually from a narrow waist to fullness concentrated about mid-thigh, where they ended; also called *gallygaskins;* used from the 16th to the 19th centuries to refer to breeches that appeared wide at the knees

smock frock: Men's knee-length, loose-fitting homespun gown; worn by farmers in the 18th century; later called *smock*

smocking: Decorative needlework from the 18th century used to hold gathered cloth together; the stitches catch alternate folds in honeycombed designs

sneakers: canvas tennis shoes

snood: A net worn as a hair covering, frequently made of colored silk or chenille; popular during the Crinoline Period and the period of World War II

soccus: A slipperlike shoe reaching to the ankle; worn in ancient Rome

solae: Simple form of sandal worn by the ancient Romans, consisting of a wooden sole held on with thongs or a cord; also called *sandalis*

soul patch: A small patch of hair centered beneath the lip

Spanish farthingale: Garment constructed of whalebone, cane, or steel hoops graduated in size from the waist to the floor and sewn into a petticoat or underskirt that provided support to the flared, cone-shaped skirt; first appeared in the mid-16th century; also called *verdugale*

Spanish work: Especially fashionable embroidery that originated in Spain and spread throughout the rest of Europe in the 16th century; consisted of delicate black silk figures worked on fine, white linen, often applied to the neck band and wrists of men's shirts and women's chemises

spatterdashers: Separate protective coverings from the 18th century that extended from the top of the shoe to some point below the knee, worn to protect the legs when sturdy shoes were worn outdoors; also called *spats*

spencer: A short jacket worn by both men and women in the 19th century that ended at the waistline; made with sleeves or sleeveless; the color usually contrasted with the rest of the costume

sport jackets: Conventional tailored jacket made in tweed, plaid, or plain colors, worn with contrasting pants for business and general wear; when these were first developed, American tailors called them casual jackets or sack jackets; the British preferred the term *lounge coat*

sportswear: Originally worn for tennis, golf, bicycling, bathing, ice skating, yachting, and hunting; now synonymous with *casual wear*

staybands: During the 17th century, thick corded or quilted material that was tied tightly around the body of children, probably intended to prevent umbilical hernias or to promote an upright posture; also called *rollers*

stays: English term for *corset*

steinkirk: A style of the cravat from the 18th century in which the tie pulled through the buttonhole and twisted loosely

step-ins: Women's underpants with widely flared legs and narrow crotch, popular in the 1920s and 1930s

stephane: Ancient Greek bridal crown

Stetson hat: Developed by John B. Stetson, after he traveled in the American West during the mid-19th century; broad-brimmed, high-crowned felt hat made of beaver and rabbit skins; cowboys adopted this practical, water-repellent, wide-brimmed, crushable hat, and Stetson began to manufacture these hats upon his return to New Jersey

stock: A linen square used in the mid-18th century that was folded to form a high neckband, stiffened with buckram, and fastened behind the neck

stola: Garment reserved for free, married women of ancient Rome that denoted status as *mater familias*; scholars disagree on its construction

stole: During the early Middle Ages, a long, narrow strip of material that clergy wore over the shoulder during the mass; after the Directoire Period, referred to shawl made in square or oblong shape; in contemporary fashion, generally refers to long narrow shawl made of any material and worn over the shoulders

stomacher: First used in men's doublets in the 16th century (also called a *paltock* in England), later with women's corsets and dresses; a garment was cut with a deep V at the front, and a filler or stomacher of contrasting color was inserted under the V, extending to the waist or beyond; separate stomachers could be tied or pinned to the front to vary the garment's appearance

straight soles: Footwear made without shaping for left or right feet

straw boater: Men's flat-topped, flat-brimmed hat with an oval crown; also worn by women for sportswear or during work; first appeared in the late 19th century

street styles: Term coined in the 20th century to describe counter-culture dress of adolescents, such as the zoot suit and the clothing worn by the Teddy Boys and the Beatniks; although street styles were intended to make a statement about being different from mainstream, these fashions also provided new ideas for the fashion industry

strophium: Female undergarment band of fabric used in ancient Rome that supported the breasts

style: The predominant form of dress of any given period or culture

subligar: Loincloth undergarment for middle- and upper-class men, and a working garment for slaves in ancient Rome

subligaria: Loincloth undergarment for women in ancient Rome; feminine form of *subligar*

sudarium: A white linen handkerchief used in ancient Rome for wiping off perspiration, veiling the face, or holding in front of the mouth to protect against disease

sumptuary laws: In Renaissance Italy, laws restricting the ownership and use of luxury goods to certain social and/or economic classes; such laws were frequently applied to clothing and its ornamentation, but were rarely obeyed or much enforced

supparum: A belted linen garment worn by young girls in ancient Rome that looked like a Greek chiton with an overfold

supportasse: Frame that supported ruffs of enormous widths during the 16th century

surcote: French word for outer tunic; more widely used than *under tunic* by costume historians when writing about periods after the 13th century

surtouts: Garments from the late 17th century with fitted straight sleeves, turned-back cuffs, and a buttoned-down front; they completely covered the breeches and waistcoat

swaddling clothes: Bands of fabric wrapped around an infant's body, thought to prevent deformity of children's limbs; common practice throughout Europe and North America until the 19th century

sweatshirt: Long-sleeved, fleece-backed, cotton knit pullover or zipped-front knit shirt made with rib-knit crew neck, rib-knit cuffs, and waistband; sometimes has attached hood and often is worn with matching sweatpants; first appeared in the 1970s

swirl skirt: A skirt made from bias-cut strips of multicolored fabrics that were often imported from India; popular in the 1970s

Swiss belt: A wide belt popular in the Crinoline Period, sometimes enclosing the rib cage, frequently laced up the front in a manner similar to a peasant's bodice

synthesis: Lightweight garment worn by men at dinner parties instead of the toga because the toga was too heavy and cumbersome to wear when the ancient Romans reclined to eat

T

T-shirt: Originally white, knit undershirts worn by men in the 1930s that featured round necks and set-in sleeves; eventually found their way into general sportswear

tabard: Originally a short, loose garment with short or no sleeves that was worn by monks and lower-class men in the early Middle Ages; in some instances, it fastened for only a short distance under the arms either by seaming or with fabric tabs; in later centuries this garment became part of military dress or the dress of servants in lordly households

tablion: Large, square decorations, in contrasting colors and fabric, that were located at the open edge over the breast on cloaks from the Byzantine Empire

tailclouts: English term for a diaper; also called *nappies*

tailor-mades: A women's garment from the 1890s for morning or country wear, usually a suit consisting of a jacket and skirt made by a tailor rather than a dressmaker

tailored dress: Pieces are cut and sewn together; they fit the body more closely and provide greater warmth than draped garments

talma mantle: A full cloak with tasseled hood or flat collar popular during the Crinoline Period

tarbush: High brimless hat shaped like a truncated cone, similar to the fez; worn in southwest Asia or northern Africa

tea gown: Long, informal hostess gown in pale colors worn from 1877 to the early 20th century; usually made of thin wool or silk, it could be worn loose-fitting and worn without a corset

tebenna: Rounded mantle worn by Etruscan men and women, woven with curved edges in a roughly semicircular or elliptical form and worn draped in various ways

teddies: Straight-cut garments of the 1920s, combining a camisole with a short slip, or long vest with underpants; a wide strap is attached to the front and back at the hem, thus making a separate opening for each leg; now refers to a one-piece tight-fitting minimal garment with a low-cut front and back and high-cut leg opening

Teddy Boys: Working-class British adolescents in the 1950s who adopted styles in menswear that had a somewhat Edwardian flavor: longer jackets with more shaping, high turned-back lapels, cuffed sleeves, waistcoats, and well-cut, narrow trousers

Tencel®: Regenerated cellulosic fiber made by a more environmentally friendly process than rayon

tête de mouton: A 18th-century women's hairstyle achieved by close, tight curls

Theatre de la Mode: An exhibit of miniature mannequins, twenty-seven inches tall, that were displayed on a miniature set in 1944 as a traveling exhibit that showed the latest fashions from the haute couture; not only featured the work of more than forty French couturiers, but also raised funds for war relief

theme: A recurring or unifying subject or idea

thong: Designed in 1975, variously described as a "virtually bottomless bathing suit" or a "glorified jockstrap," cut to reveal as much of the buttocks as possible while covering the crotch; now a common cut for underwear

tippet: Narrow fur or feather piece from the 18th century that was worn around the shoulders like a modern-day stole

toga: Semicircular draped garment symbolizing Roman citizenship, worn by men and free Roman children; see *toga praetexta* for toga used by children

toga candida: Toga lightened to an exceptional white shade and worn by candidates for office in ancient Rome; the word *candidate* derives from this term

toga picta: Purple toga with gold embroidery, assigned on special occasions to victorious generals or other persons in ancient Rome who distinguished themselves in some way

toga praetexta: Toga with a purple border worn by the young sons (until age 16) and daughters (until age 12) of the ancient Roman nobility and by certain adult magistrates and high priests

toga pulla: Black or dark-colored toga, said to have been worn for mourning in ancient Rome

toga pura: Plain white, undecorated wool toga worn after the age of 16 by the ordinary male ancient Roman citizen

toga trabea: Multicolored, striped toga assigned to augurs (religious officials who prophesied the future) or important officials in ancient Rome

toga virilis: See *toga pura*

toga with folded bands: Style in which the overfold was folded back-and-forth upon itself until a folded band of fabric was formed at the top of the semicircle

tonsure: Distinctive haircut worn by priests in the early Middle Ages

topcoat: A type of lightweight overcoat

top hat: Men's tall hat made of shiny silk or beaver cloth with a narrow brim; first developed toward the end of the 18th century as part of men's riding costume; was the predominant hat style during the Directoire Period, and remained so throughout the rest of the 19th century

topper coat: Woman's hip-length coat, often made with a flared silhouette, popular in the early 1940s

toque: High brimless hat especially popular in the early 19th century

toupee: 18th-century French term for brushing the hair straight back from the forehead and into a slightly elevated roll; also called a *foretop*

trapeze: Unfitted dress with narrow shoulders that gradually grows to a very wide hem, somewhat like a pyramid; introduced in the late 1950s

trench coat: A water-repellent coat of closely woven cotton twill, belted at the waist; became a standard item for men after World War I, and after several decades, was also adopted by women

trilby: Man's soft felt hat with supple brim

trickle down theory of fashion: The idea that fashion changes result from the initial adoption of new and innovative styles by the upper socio-economic classes, and the subsequent imitation of these styles by the lower socio-economic classes; see also *bottom-up theory of fashion*

tricorne: Term coined by costume historians for a variation of the cocked men's hat, turned up to form three equidistant peaks with one peak in the center front; worn in the 18th century

trousers: In modern usage, a bifurcated (two-legged) garment worn by men or women; term sometimes used interchangeably with *pantaloons*; in early 19th century, usually close-fitting pants for men with an ankle strap or slit that laced to fit the ankle

trucker's cap: A variation of the baseball cap that had a foam section at the front of the crown and mesh around the rest of the cap

trunk hose: Breeches worn by men in the mid-16th century that were joined to nether stocks; ranged in size from very wide and padded to very small and worn with tight-fitting hose

tuckers: See *chemisettes*

tunic: Simple, one-piece, and often T-shaped garments with openings for the head and the arms; usually long enough to cover the torso; in contemporary usage, for women's clothing often means an upper layer of at least hip length worn over pants or a skirt

tunic suit: A 19th-century jacket fitted to the waist, attached to a full, gathered, or pleated skirt that ended at the knee; buttoned down the front, often had a wide belt; usually worn with trousers; some versions for small boys ages 3 to 6 combined the tunic jacket with frilled, white drawers

turban: Traditionally, a men headdress consisting of a long scarf of linen, cotton, or silk wound around a small cap or directly around the head; in more recent times, a woman's version is a close-fitting hat material wound around a small inner cap or a hat constructed to look like a man's or woman's turban.

Turkish trousers: Pants with full legs gathered to fit tightly at the ankle; worn under short skirts to create the "bloomer" costume, which was developed by American feminists in the late 19th century to reform women's clothes of the period, which they saw as confining and impractical; named after Amelia Bloomer, who endorsed the style, wrote favorably about it in 1851 in a journal she edited, and wore it for lectures

turtleneck jersey: Gained popularity for a time as a substitute for shirts and ties when, in 1924, actor Noel Coward initiated the style; popular again in the 1960s and after

tutulus: A high-crowned, small-brimmed hat worn by the Etruscans; in ancient Rome, referred to a special hairstyle where the hair is drawn to the top of the head and wrapped in *vittae*, designating the status of *mater familias*

tweens: A new segment of the children's market—ages 7 to 14—that emerged by the 2000s

twin set: Matching cardigan sweater and pullover sweater

U

ulster: A long, almost ankle-length men's or women's coat from the late 19th century with a full or half belt and sometimes a detachable hood or cape

umbo: Created by pulling a clump of fabric up from the first and invisible part of the Roman toga that had been placed vertically from floor to shoulder; may have helped to hold the toga drapery in place, but seems ultimately to have become a decorative element

union suits: Combinations used by men and women in the late 19th century that united drawers and under-vests into one garment popular

unisex clothing: Garments first appearing in the late 1980s designed to be worn by either men or women

unitard: A one-piece bodysuit from 1980s made of patterned, knitted fabric that combines leotards and tights into one suit

upper stocks: Section of men's hose that in the 16th century was sewn together with the nether stocks; eventually took on the appearance of a separate garment, and was cut somewhat fuller than the lower section; see also *breeches*

upsweep: Popular 1940s woman's hairstyle with medium-long hair brushed upward from the sides and nape of neck, then secured on top of the head in curls or a pompadour

uraeus: Sacred cobra, symbol of Lower Egypt in antiquity

V

veil: Cloth rectangle, smaller than either a shawl or a cloak, worn by women to cover the head and sometimes part of the body

Venetians: Skintight version of breeches from the late 16th century, wide at the top and tapering to the knee

verdugado: See *Spanish farthingale*

verdugale: See *Spanish farthingale*

vest: Garment adopted by King Charles II of England in 1666 that consisted of a knee-length outer coat, and a waistcoat of the same length that obscured the beeches beneath; in subsequent centuries, referred to the combination of an outer coat (the cut of which varied), a sleeved or sleeveless waistcoat (of varying lengths), and breeches or trousers that became a basic costume for men; in contemporary fashion, refers to a sleeveless garment, buttoned down the front, and usually worn over a shirt or a blouse, and if part of a three-piece suit, worn under the outer jacket

Victoria sleeve: A variation of the sleeve en bouffant with a puff at the elbow; popular during the Victorian Period

vintage clothing: Term coined in the late 20th century for clothes and accessories from another fashion period refurbished and sold in department stores or specialty shops

virago sleeves: Stylish sleeves that were paned and tied into a series of puffs, popular during the 17th century

virtual Internet sites: Internet sites consisting of imaginary environments that participants can develop and where they can create a character representing themselves, called an *avatar*

vitta: A woolen band used by matrons in ancient Rome to bind hair; plural *vittae*

W

waistcoat: See *vest*

walking dress: See *day dress*

walking shorts: Based on military costume of British Colonial soldiers, adopted in the 1930s by the well-to-do for vacation wear, revived in the 1950s as general sportswear for men and women; also called *Bermuda shorts*

Wallace Beery shirt: See *Henley shirt*

warp: Yarns that run lengthwise in woven fabric

wash-and-wear: Easy-to-care-for fabrics that did not require ironing, first developed in the late 1950s

wash ball: A combination of rice powder, flour, starch, white lead, and orris root used in place of soap during the 18th century

Watteau back: A 19th-century term for loose-fitting, pleated-back styles of the type called *robe à l'Anglaise* in the 18th century

wearable art: Beginning in the 1970s, a garment created as a unique work of art; Fiber artists combine a variety of techniques such as crocheting, hand-weaving, and slashing, as well as feathers, beads, and ribbons

wedge: Cut in which the hair is tapered close to the head at the nape of the neck, above this the hair is full and all one length; the front and sides are all one length, squared off at the middle of the ear, and short bangs are informally styled; became popular in 1976 after Olympic medal–winner Dorothy Hamill wore the style at the Olympic games

weejuns: Moccasin-type shoes introduced in the 1930s, adapted from shoes worn by Norwegian fishermen

weft: See *filling*

weighting: A process used to give silk fabric greater body, in which silk was treated with metallic salts; first used in the late 1870s; excessive weighting damaged fabrics, and by the late 1930s, legislation set limits on how much weighting could be added

Western dress: Style of dress prevalent in Western Europe and Euro-America since the Middle Ages

western shirt: See *cowboy shirt*

wheel farthingale: *See French farthingale*

wheelys: Shoes from the 2000s with wheels set into the soles

whisk: A wide lace collar or band of linen from the late 17th century

white bucks: White buckskin shoes whose popularity in the 1950s is directly attributable to television

white crown: Worn by Egyptian pharaohs to symbolize rule over Upper Egypt

wide awake: A cap with a low crown and wide brim and made of felt or straw, popular during the Crinoline Period

wifebeaters: Tops cut like men's athletic shirts; Marlon Brando wore one when he played a violent working-class husband in the play and film *A Streetcar Named Desire*

wimple: A fine white linen or silk scarf from the early Middle Ages that covered the neck; the center was placed under the chin and each end pulled up and fastened above the ear or at the temple; generally worn in combination with a veil

winkle pickers: Men's shoes with exaggeratedly pointed toes; popular with the Teddy Boys from the 1950s

winter mantles: From the early Middle Ages, mantles for outdoor wear; could be lined with fur

woad: Readily available natural blue dye used in the Middle Ages by peasants on their coarse clothing

wrapped skirt: In ancient cultures, cloth wrapped around the waist; major garment for men in Egyptian history, with length, width, and fit dependent on time period and social class; in Minoan culture, worn by both men and women; in Egypt, also called *shent* or *skent*; see also *skirt*

Y

yuppie: A nickname from the 1980s applied to young, upwardly mobile professionals who work in fields such as law and business; male yuppies wore Italian double-breasted "power suits" to work, and female yuppies donned similarly cut women's versions

Z

zeitgeist: The specific expression of an era determined by a complex mixture of social, psychological, and aesthetic factors; spirit of the times

zip-in lining: A feature from the 1930s that made cold-weather coats convertible to be used in warmer temperatures

zipper: A toothed slide fastener first mass-produced in the 1920s by B. F. Goodrich; adjective used to describe apparel in which a zipper is a prominent feature

zoot suit: An extreme form of the sack suit with a long jacket, excessively wide shoulders, wide lapels, and markedly pegged trousers; originated in the 1940s, some say with Mexican-American immigrant workers (called *pachucos*) in southern California, while others claim it was first worn by an African-American bus driver in Gainesville, Georgia

zouave: Short, collarless jacket, trimmed with braid and often worn over a Garibaldi shirt during the Crinoline Period

NOTES AND SKETCHES

NOTES AND SKETCHES

NOTES AND SKETCHES